early years
aining &
nagement

Gaining your NVQ Level 2 in Early Years Care and Education

Meg Jones

Editor	**Author**	**Illustrations**
Sarah Sodhi	Meg Jones	Simon Rumble/Beehive Illustration
Assistant Editor	**Series Designer**	**Cover artwork**
Helen Watts	Mark Udall	© Martyn Chillmaid
	Designer	
	Catherine Mason	

Acknowledgements
Her Majesty's Stationery Office and Queen's Printer for Scotland for the use of materials from *NVQ in Early Years Care and Education* produced by the Care Sector Consortium with funding from the Department for Education and Employment © 2000, Crown copyright.

Every effort has been made to trace copyright holders and the publishers apologise for any inadvertent omissions.

Text © 2003 Meg Jones
© 2003 Scholastic Ltd

Designed using Adobe PageMaker

Published by Scholastic Ltd, Villiers House,
Clarendon Avenue, Leamington Spa, Warwickshire CV32 5PR

Visit our website at www.scholastic.co.uk

Printed by Bell & Bain Ltd. Glasgow

1 2 3 4 5 6 7 8 9 0   3 4 5 6 7 8 9 0 1 2

Contents

Introduction   **5**

C1 Support children's physical development needs   **11**

C1.1 Help children to toilet and wash hands   *11*

C1.2 Help children when eating and drinking   *13*

C1.3 Support opportunities for children's exercise   *15*

C1.4 Support children's quiet periods   *17*

C4 Support children's social and emotional development   **20**

C4.1 Help children to adjust to new settings   *20*

C4.2 Help children to relate to others   *22*

C4.3 Help children to develop self-reliance and self-esteem   *24*

C4.4 Help children to recognise and deal with their feelings   *26*

C4.5 Assist children to develop positive aspects of their behaviour   *28*

C8 Implement planned activities for sensory and intellectual development   **32**

C8.1 Provide activities, equipment and materials for creative play   *32*

C8.2 Play games with children   *34*

C8.3 Assist children with cooking activities   *35*

C8.4 Provide opportunities and equipment for manipulative play   *38*

C8.5 Examine objects of interest with children   *40*

C9 Implement planned activities for the development of language and communication skills   **44**

C9.1 Implement music sessions   *44*

C9.2 Implement and participate in talking and listening activities   *46*

C9.3 Select and use equipment and materials to stimulate role-play   *48*

C9.4 Select and diaplay books   *50*

C9.5 Relate stories and rhymes   *52*

E1 Maintain an attractive, stimulating and reassuring environment for children   **56**

E1.1 Maintain the physical environment   *56*

E1.2 Prepare and maintain displays   *58*

E1.3 Maintain a reassuring environment   *60*

E2 Maintain the safety and security of children   **63**

E2.1 Maintain a safe environment for children   *63*

E2.2 Maintain the supervision of children   *65*

E2.3 Carry out emergency procedures   *67*

E2.4 Cope with accidents and injuries to children   *69*

E2.5 Help protect children from abuse   *70*

E2.6 Maintain the safety of children on outings   *72*

M3 Contribute to the achievement of organisational requirements   **76**

M3.1 Carry out instructions and provide feedback   *76*

M3.2 Contribute to the development of good practice   *78*

P1 Relate to parents   **81**

P1.1 Interact and share information with parents about their children   *81*

P1.2 Share the care of children with their parents   *83*

Contents

C12 Feed babies   **87**

C12.1 Prepare equipment and formula feed   *87*

C12.2 Feed babies by bottle   *89*

C12.3 Prepare food and feed babies   *91*

C13 Provide for babies' physical developmental needs   **94**

C13.1 Wash babies   *94*

C13.2 Change nappies and dress babies   *96*

C13.3 Encourage development through stimulation   *97*

C13.4 Clean and maintain clothing and nursery equipment   *99*

M1 Monitor, store and prepare materials and equipment   **102**

M1.1 Prepare equipment   *102*

M1.2 Prepare materials   *104*

M1.3 Monitor and store materials   *106*

P9 Work with parents in a group   **109**

P9.1 Inform parents about the operation of the group   *109*

P9.2 Encourage parents to participate in group functions   *111*

P9.3 Encourage parents to participate in children's activities   *113*

CU10 Contribute to the effectiveness of work teams   **116**

CU10.1 Contribute to effective team working   *116*

CU10.2 Develop oneself in own work role   *118*

Photocopiable pages   **121**

Activity preparation   *121*

Spider chart   *122*

Behaviour game   *123*

Hop frog hop   *124*

Easy recipes   *125*

Play dough recipes   *126*

A walk in the woods   *127*

Menu   *128*

Story aids   *129*

Setting checklist   *130*

Round robin   *131*

999   *132*

Skeleton   *133*

Tips for naming names   *134*

Play activities   *135*

Baby games   *136*

Baby menu   *137*

Equipment checklist   *138*

Cinema role-play   *139*

Greeting card   *140*

Notice   *141*

Meeting plan   *142*

Action plan   *143*

Reflective account   *144*

Introduction

Taking an NVQ can be a daunting experience until you become familiar with the system and used to the language. However it is a very practical way to gain a nationally recognised qualification that you can complete in your regular work setting. An NVQ Level 2 in Early Years Care and Education qualifies you to work in a supporting role, working in a supervised position with children up to the age of eight years, in a range of settings.

You will need to prepare yourself for the practical aspects, demonstrate your understanding and knowledge of childcare and early years, and provide evidence of your work in a portfolio (a file) to the satisfaction of your assessor. The outcome is a qualification comparable to other recognised courses for supervised positions with young children. This book will help you to collect the evidence for the practical aspects you will need to undertake.

Following registration with an NVQ assessment centre you will be given a candidate's copy of the *Guidance* and the *National Occupational Standards for Early Years Care and Education Level 2*. These detail the areas you need to cover, which are the same for all the awarding bodies. You will also be allocated an assessor, who will observe you at your work setting to ensure you are meeting the Standards. Working towards an NVQ is a two-way process between you and your assessor, who will have an early years background. Your assessor will explain what is required, help you to understand the terminology and guide you through the process. However you have to do the work!

The Unit approach

An NVQ is presented in Units. A Level 2 qualification consists of eight mandatory Units, plus two optional Units, from a choice of five. Throughout the process the NVQ is broken down into detail, to ensure everything is covered. Each Unit consists of a number of Elements addressing different aspects. Each Element presents a range of situations and the performance criteria that need to be demonstrated, either in direct work with the children or by some other form, in order to meet the Standards. You can work your way through each Unit, but as life and learning does not come in neat categories, evidence presented for one Unit should be cross-referenced to others. Although this appears complicated

and will take you some time to fully understand, you can be assured that you will eventually grasp the concept. Remember you are not on your own, your assessor will help you.

This book suggests ideas and activities for each of the eight mandatory Units, on an Element-by-Element basis, plus the five optional Units.

Mandatory Units

C1	Support children's physical development needs.
C4	Support children's social and emotional development.
C8	Implement planned activities for sensory and intellectual development.
C9	Implement planned activities for the development of language and communication skills.
E1	Maintain an attractive, stimulating and reassuring environment for children.
E2	Maintain the safety and security of children.
M3	Contribute to the achievement of organisational requirements.
P1	Relate to parents.

Optional Units

C12	Feed babies.
C13	Provide for babies' physical development needs.
M1	Monitor, store and prepare materials and equipment.
P9	Work with parents in a group.
CU10	Contribute to the effectiveness of work teams.

Within your Standards ...

➤ You will see the titles listed above. These are the **Units**.

➤ Under each heading are between two and six sub-headings. These are the **Elements**.

➤ In each Element there are up to 14 **Performance Criteria**, referred to as PCs. These are the factors you have to demonstrate to prove your capability to work at the required standard.

➤ In a box by the Performance Criteria are the **Range** statements. The Range may cover children with and without difficulties, with and without special needs, indoors and outdoors, different methods, types of play, concepts and so on. Identified within each Unit are those areas that must be directly observed by your assessor, those that may be observed by a witness and those that you have to provide evidence for.

➤ Numbers and letters provide **quick references** to Units, Elements, and Performance Criteria. For example C1 'Support children's physical development needs' is often referred to just as C1. The first Element in C1 is 'Help children to toilet and wash hands', so this is referred to as C1.1. The third Performance Criterion for this area is 'Children are allowed sufficient time to complete toileting and hand washing', and this is referred to as C1.1: 3.

➤ The **evidence** is the record of *direct observations* of you working with the children and *witness testimonies* signed by your colleagues when the assessor is not there. *Work products* can include copies of children's records, menus, charts, forms from your setting, letters and information to parents and carers, and examples of the children's work. *Child observations* and *reflective accounts* are your own accounts of what happened, how you dealt with it and an evaluation. Always ensure that children cannot be identified from any records you use in your portfolio. In addition, your supporting evidence can include *curriculum plans*, an *inspection* report of the setting, *diaries*, *log books* and *notes* recording everyday incidents, *case studies*, *assignments* and *simulations*, for example, when you are unable to get evidence for an emergency evacuation or a sick child. You can also be *questioned*. This can be both written and spoken (although both need to be recorded in writing for the portfolio). Any *training* you undertake during an NVQ or a *prior achievement*, such as first aid or food hygiene, can be included. It must be recent; you must provide a certificate or letter of confirmation and a copy of the syllabus; and your assessor will question you on the relevant aspects. Your assessment centre will provide further details about this.

➤ You will need to demonstrate **knowledge and understanding** of what you are doing with the children. You can do this through your actions, questioning by your assessor, assignments and case studies. There is a page at the end of each Unit indicating what you need to know. You will be expected to attend training to underpin knowledge, read books and childcare magazines, and undertake your own research as required. Copies of magazine articles, policies prepared by others and photocopies of handouts are not evidence, but you can be questioned on them, which is evidence.

➤ The **setting** is a generic word used to mean any place of work with young children where you will be assessed.

➤ Your assessor will work with you to produce **assessment plans** as an ongoing record of your progress. These also need to be included in your portfolio.

➤ Although you will probably work through the Units one or two at a time, it is preferable to take a **holistic** view. This means addressing more than one aspect at the same time. Life does not come in neat categories. If the children are playing in the home corner they will be communicating, developing self-esteem, reflecting their culture, developing fine motor skills, and displaying positive or unwanted behaviour. You will be interacting, communicating, aware of safety issues and reinforcing positive behaviour. This is a holistic approach.

➤ The **curriculum** refers to the range of activities and experiences offered to the children. To be effective you need to plan the activity, detail what the children will gain from it and evaluate it afterwards.

➤ You will come across the term **cross-reference** in any NVQ documentation. This means that even though you may have planned an activity for one area, such as C8.3 'Assist children with cooking activities', your assessor will also note how you deal with other areas, such as positive and negative behaviour (C4.4 and C4.5), reinforcing language development and introducing new words (C9.2). So one activity will produce evidence for a number of Units. You will need to assess each piece of evidence in your portfolio to see where it can be cross-referenced. It takes time to do this, as you need to know what is in the Standards, but your assessor will help you.

➤ In addition to the Performance Criteria identified in each Unit you are expected to conform to the **principles of good practice**. These are described in the NVQ Guidance and below.

➤ Your assessor will directly observe you to ensure you are carrying out the requirements with competence. If there are gaps in your knowledge or you need more practice, your assessor will suggest ways to gain the necessary evidence.

➤ Your assessor will give you regular **feedback** on your progress.

➤ You need to provide at least three different types of evidence in each Unit. When you meet the Standards your assessor will sign your work off and declare that competence has been met.

➤ Make sure all the evidence you have produced has your **signature** on it to confirm it is your own work. Your assessor will also sign and date it.

➤ Once a Unit is completed it is submitted to the assessment centre for **internal verification**. A trained verifier, who knows the Standards well and who may also be an assessor, checks that all the necessary documentation is in place and that there is sufficient, reliable and recent evidence in your portfolio to judge your competence.

The principles of good practice

These statements are based on the current legislation and guidance, including the United Nations Convention on the Rights of the Child, the Children Act 1989, relevant curricula and accepted good practice. Strands of the principles should permeate throughout the NVQ. The relevant principles are listed at the front of each Unit. These must be put into practice for you to meet the requirements of the NVQ.

1 The welfare of the child

All practical work with children should give a high priority to their welfare. Children have a right to quality care in a safe environment, to be treated with respect by caring adults, to be listened to and to be protected from harm. Children must never be shaken, smacked, slapped or ridiculed. Demonstrate that children are the focus of your thinking in your work and portfolio.

2 Keeping children safe

Children need protecting from the environment and abuse by adults. You must be aware of the safety implications when children are taking part in activities and at all other times. For example, when planning outdoor play, do a risk assessment on the area, the equipment, supervision and potential hazards. Children should be kept safe and their health protected, this includes accurate record-keeping and emergency procedures.

3 Working in partnership with parents/families

You need to recognise that parents and carers are children's first educators. Together practitioners and parents can offer the best developmental support for children, by sharing information. Respect must be given to children from different backgrounds and traditions, and parents' wishes taken into consideration. Record the children's developmental progress and share your thoughts and observations with the parents.

4 Children's learning and development

The majority of activities offered in an under-eights setting can be used as a learning experience. Children should be offered a wide range of experiences and activities, including physical, intellectual, emotional, social, communication and spiritual. For example, when you plan for water play consider the gross motor skills of lifting and pouring, the mathematical concepts of volume and measurement, the scientific aspects of floating and sinking, the emotional benefit of self-reliance and satisfaction, the behaviour management (not splashing others) and communication through interaction with peers. Have learning objectives for each lesson or activity and evaluate it afterwards.

5 Equality of opportunity

Every child should have an equal chance of accessing all opportunities for learning and development. The aim is for all children to reach their full potential and that means treating each child as an individual. Avoid stereotyping and consider the cultural implications of each activity you organise. Look at your plans critically. Do they exclude children with special needs? How could you adapt them to be inclusive? Widen your knowledge by studying the impact of disability and the cultural backgrounds of all the children. Equality of opportunity extends to cover family members and colleagues.

6 Anti-discrimination

Every person working in early years care and education must ensure that no one is discriminated against on the grounds of gender, racial origins, religion, culture, social background, disability, class, family unit or sexual orientation. Consider how you would challenge discriminatory language between children.

7 Celebrating diversity

We live in a multicultural, multilingual, multifaith, multiracial society. This should be reflected in your work regardless of whether you have children from minority ethnic groups in your setting or children for whom English is an additional language. Consider whether your setting visually reflects cultural diversity. Children need to develop a sense of identity within their cultural background and to learn about cultures different to their own. We all have a culture and this should be respected.

8 Confidentiality

Every setting should have a policy on confidentiality. Never discuss information about children, families or colleagues outside work. Find out about the confidentiality policy in your setting. Do not present evidence in your portfolio that can be used to identify children. Use a fictitious name or code, or simply omit the name. If you use a fictitious name, make this clear on the document so the assessors and verifiers know it is not genuine.

9 Working with other professionals

Always remember you are not working alone. When unsure and where appropriate, seek advice from others who are more experienced than yourself. Working as part of a team is a vital element in quality childcare. Respect other professionals. Be a good team worker.

10 The reflective practitioner

Be prepared to look back over your work, seek advice from your supervisor, accept further training and develop your skills throughout your period of work with the children and their families.

Using the book

This book is designed to offer a range of activities and ideas to cover all the practical aspects of the NVQ in Early Years Care and Education Level 2. It does not include underpinning knowledge that would need to be gained from other sources.

There is a main activity for each Element, a case study, questions, tips, a 'Did you know?' slot and extra ideas. Indications are given as to which Range statement or Performance Criteria may be met, but this is not exclusive. When you complete activities sometimes you will cover them all, other times you will miss some out. Your assessor may identify further ones not stated here. Every candidate will operate differently. At the end of each Unit there are 'answer pointers', which are key words in random order. They are not intended to be everything you can say about a subject but just enough to get you started. It is intended that the answers should be written out in full.

At the end of the book are a number of photocopiable sheets. These are included to help you in the process of gaining your NVQ. There are back-up pages to support suggested activities and sample forms for recording plans, observations and children's development, for example. NVQs require a flexible approach. There are no set forms, so you may choose to use the forms used by your setting or the ones included here. It is important that you use planning sheets to show you have thought through the whole planning process, that you offer a balanced curriculum,

that learning objectives have been identified, the preparation required has been thought through and you have evaluated activities offered.

You will not need to do everything in this book to gain the qualification. By taking a holistic approach, one activity could cover a number of different Units and Elements. If you plan carefully to incorporate as much variety as possible, during one direct observation, you can be very time efficient. This book will give you choice.

Gaining an NVQ is not the easy option and it does not suit everyone. There is a lot of work to be done, a mass of paperwork to be organised and a whole new language to learn. By the end of the NVQ you will have covered every aspect of early years care and education, will have honed your skills, and learned a great deal. This is just the start – good luck!

C1 Support children's physical development needs

This Unit covers the support of children's physical development needs in a variety of settings where children are cared for individually or in groups.

This chapter will enable you to:
C1.1 Help children to toilet and wash hands
C1.2 Help children when eating and drinking
C1.3 Support opportunities for children's exercise
C1.4 Support children's quiet periods.

Element C1.1 Help children to toilet and wash hands

➤ Your assessor can observe and question you. · · · · · · · · · · · · · · · · · · · **C1.1**: Range 1a, b, 2a, b ◄

Hand border
Number of children: four.

Resources
Large sheets of sugar paper; tray for paint; ready-mixed paint; bowl of soapy water; paper towels; scissors; glue or stapler; wipe-clean cover for table; aprons; display area.

Preparation
Plan the activity using the 'Activity preparation' photocopiable sheet on page 121. Ask your setting supervisor for support in doing this if necessary. Protect the table. Squeeze a thin layer of paint into the tray. Have soapy water and towels close by. Help the children put their aprons on.

What to do
➤ Discuss the importance of washing hands. Can the children suggest when to wash hands, such as after using the toilet and before eating.
➤ Invite the children to make a collage of their hand prints.
➤ Let the children press their hands flat in the paint and on to the sugar paper a few times, leaving space around each print.
➤ Encourage the children to wash and dry their hands.
➤ Help the children carefully cut out the prints.
➤ Staple the hands around the edge of the display, leaving the fingers fluttering.

Tip

➤ Each time you plan an activity complete an 'Activity preparation' sheet (see page 121). This will ensure you are clear about what you are doing, who you are doing it with and what resources you need to have.
➤ To encourage potty training, start when the child is ready, praise any success and expect accidents.

Support and extension

Help younger children to cut out the hand prints. Challenge older children to make elaborate designs for the display.

Evaluation

Although a fun activity, hand washing is a serious subject. Do you think you got the message across well?

Supporting activity

Collect hand-washing posters to share with the children from your local Health Promotion Department. Suggest that the children make their own posters to promote hand washing to other children. Display these with the hand print border.

➤ **C1.1**: *1, 2, 3, 7, 9, 10*

Case study

Abigail is three and has occasional 'toilet' accidents, which she finds distressing. Her mum is concerned that Abigail may be excluded if it becomes a nuisance to the setting. You have been asked to observe Abigail, to deal with any accidents and report any concerns or progress to the supervisor. What could the causes be and how will you deal with the situation to reassure Abigail and her mum? Write down the case study with your responses for your portfolio.

➤ **C1.1**: *1, 2, 3, 8, 9, 10*

Follow on

Consider how to introduce potty training and what emotional, health, hygiene and safety issues to address. Write up your notes, discuss with your assessor and put in your portfolio.

Questions

(See answer pointers at end of chapter.)

➤ **C1.1**: *2* · · · · · · · · · · · **1.** *How can you develop self-reliance in toileting and hand washing?*

➤ **C1.1**: *5* · · · · · · · · · **2.** *What are the health education and body awareness issues that you can discuss during hand washing and toileting?*

➤ **C1.1**: *6* · · · · · · · · **3.** *What signs and symptoms, suggesting infection and abuse, can you check during toileting and hand washing?*

Record the questions and your full answers and share these with your assessor.

Did you know?

On average, an adult has two colds a year and a child has four. Remember, a sneeze spreads millions of germs and only a few are needed to spread a cold. Dispose of tissues and wash hands regularly.

Extra idea

➤ **C1.1**: *10* · · · · · · · Demonstrate your hand-washing techniques to your assessor after helping the children to use the toilet.

Element C1.2 Help children when eating and drinking

➤ Your assessor can observe and question you. . . . . **C1.2**: *Range 1a, b, c, 2a, b, 3a* ◄

Snack time sandwiches

Number of children: four.

Resources

Sliced wholemeal loaf; sliced white loaf; butter; Marmite; jam; banana; cheese spread or hard cheese and grater; tomato; brown sugar; four plates; four blunt knives; small bowl; fork; round pastry cutters; aprons.

✓ **Tip**

➤ Keep a clean cloth handy to mop up any spills.

C1.2: 7

Preparation

Plan the activity using the 'Activity preparation' photocopiable sheet on page 121. Ask your setting supervisor for support in doing this if necessary. Clean the surface, put on an apron and wash your hands. Place the ingredients in the centre of the table. Check for any food allergies or dietary requirements.

What to do

➤ Encourage the children to wash their hands and put on clean aprons.
➤ Talk to the children about their food likes and dislikes.
➤ Let the children choose brown or white bread, or one of each.
➤ Show the children how to spread the butter on two slices of bread each.
➤ Cut each slice of bread in half and invite the children to choose two sandwich fillings.
➤ Help the children to spread the sandwich fillings on one half of the bread. If using banana, encourage the children to squash the banana in the bowl with a fork. Place the second slice of bread on top and press down gently.
➤ Using the pastry cutter, show the children how to cut two circles out of the bread.
➤ Invite the children to decorate the top of their savoury sandwiches with a smiley face made from a processed cheese mouth and attach little pieces of tomatoes for eyes with a dab of cheese spread. Sprinkle a small amount of sugar over the sweet sandwiches.

Support and extension

➤ *Cross-reference to* **C8** · · Help young children to make their sandwiches. Allow older children to make the ◄ sandwiches with minimal assistance. Depending on ability, the more able children may, with supervision, be able to grate the hard cheese. Use different-shaped cutters and additional decorations to make fancy sandwiches.

Evaluation

Were you well prepared? Were the children willing to try different fillings? Did you encourage them to be adventurous? Did the children prefer brown or white bread? What alternative fillings can you suggest? Did the children enjoy eating their sandwiches at snack time?

Supporting activity

➤ **C1.2**: *1* · · · · · · · · Investigate what it means to have a balanced diet. Collect leaflets from the Health ◄ Promotion Department and write up what constitutes a healthy diet for children. Consider diets from different cultures.

➤ **C1.2**: *1, 7, 8* · · · · · ·
Case study
You have been told that Yasmin is allergic to peanuts. One day you see her ◄ swapping her food with another child. You know this could be an emergency situation. What can you do and who will you tell? Write down the case study with your responses for your portfolio.

Follow on
Find out what can happen to a child who is allergic to certain foods. Find out which foods most commonly affect children. Draw up a menu for a child who has Coeliac Disease and tell your assessor about this condition.

Questions
(See answer pointers at end of chapter.)

➤ **C1.2**: *2, 3* · · · · · · · **4.** *How can you make eating and drinking more enjoyable and encourage self-* ◄ *reliance in young children?*

➤ **C1.2**: *4* · · · · · · · · · **5.** *What equipment and protective clothing helps young children and children with* ◄ *special needs to feed themselves?*

➤ **C1.2**: *5* · · · · · · · · · **6.** *What are the cultural considerations regarding acceptable behaviour at home* ◄ *that you need to know relating to eating and drinking?*

Record the questions and your full answers and share these with your assessor.

Did you know?
Young children should never be put on a slimming diet. If overweight, their diet needs to be controlled by sticking to three meals a day with healthy snacks in between. Portion control of appropriate foods, high calorie sweet foods kept as a treat and energetic play and exercise will keep the child healthy until they grow into their excess weight.

Extra ideas

➤ **C1.2**: *1* · · · · · · · · Using the 'Spider chart' photocopiable sheet on page 121, write 'A healthy diet' ◄ in the centre. In each of the surrounding boxes identify the food groups and give examples suitable for young children.

➤ **C1.2**: *5* · · · · · · · · Provide cooking pots, stainless steel cups and chopsticks in the home corner. ◄

Element C1.3 Support opportunities for children's exercise

➤ Your assessor can observe and question you. · · · · · · · · · · · · · · · ·

C1.3: *Range 1a, b, 2a, b, c, d, 3a, b* ◄

Playground games

Encouraging children to be active is an important aspect of early years work. Playing games is a fun way to exercise.
Number of children: small group.

Resources

Large ball; open space.

What to do

➤ Invite the children to play 'What's the time Mr Wolf?'. Pretend to be Mr Wolf and walk ahead of a row of children. Invite the children to chant 'What's the time Mr Wolf?'. Explain to the children that they have to tiptoe very quietly behind Mr Wolf. At random intervals turn around quickly to face the children and tell them a time, such as 'one o'clock' or 'seven o'clock'. Let the children creep closer and closer. Then, instead of calling out a time, say 'dinner time' and chase the children back to the start. On the way back, try to catch one of the children and explain that it is now their turn to be Mr Wolf.

➤ Gather the children and invite them to play 'Here we go round the mulberry bush' (Traditional).

♦ Encourage the children to hold hands, skip around in a circle and sing the chorus. At the end of each verse stop and do the actions. Begin by using the actions the children are familiar with, such as 'This is the way we clean our teeth', '... brush our hair' and '... stamp our feet'.

♦ Sing the song together and encourage the children to extend the game by adding in their own actions, such as 'This is the way we go to sleep', '... polish our shoes' and '... sweep the floor'.

➤ Play 'Ring-o-ring-o-roses' on grass with very small children.

➤ Invite the children to spread out into a large circle to play a ball game. Explain that you are going to throw the ball at someone and they must catch it. When it is their turn to catch the ball, the children must choose someone else in the circle and throw it to them. Ensure that everyone gets a turn.

➤ Suggest playing 'The hokey cokey' with the children. Invite the children to form a circle and do the actions while singing the song:

'You put your left foot in, your left foot out,
In, out, in, out and shake it all about.
You do the hokey cokey and you turn around.
That's what it's all about.'

When it comes to the chorus encourage all the children to hold hands and rush into the centre of the circle while singing:

'Ohhh ... the hokey cokey.
Ohhh ... the hokey cokey.
Ohhh ... the hokey cokey.
That's what it's all about.'

✔ Tip

➤ If you see a child hit by a ball check they have not been injured before carrying on.

C1.3: *12*

Continue singing all the the verses of 'The Hokey Cokey' together, using all the parts of the body.
➤ Make up a game of 'Follow the leader'. Use all the available space and make it as active as possible.

Support and extension

➤ *Cross-reference to* **C8** · · Choose active games suitable for the developmental level of the children. Ensure ◄ your games are inclusive so that all the children can take part, even if this means you need to change the rules. Encourage the children to listen to instructions, take turns and co-operate with one another.

Evaluation

Did the children enjoy playing the games? Which games did they enjoy the most? Did you feel confident introducing and playing the games? What do you think the children got out of the activity? Were they physically active? Did you make good use of the space available?

Supporting activity

➤ *Cross-reference to* **C8** · · Keep a notebook with a record of all the games you know. When you come ◄ across a new game or idea, add it to your collection. You can categorise under various headings, such as outdoor games, indoor games, ball games, games needing equipment, games without equipment and party games.

Case study

➤ **C1.3**: *1, 6, 7, 8, 9* · · · You have noticed that the boys always race for the bikes when the children ◄ go outside to play. You are concerned because, as the boys dominate this play, the girls are less active as they tend to play in the sand. How can you ensure both boys and girls have an equal chance to play with all the equipment? Write down the case study with your responses for your portfolio.

Follow on

➤ **C1.3**: *1, 3, 6, 7, 8, 9* · · Watch the children playing and make a note of it in your notebook. Do the ◄ boys always play with certain toys and equipment? Do the girls always play with certain toys and equipment? Do they play with the same equipment but use it differently? Consider how you can encourage all children to play with a range of equipment, particularly those that promote active play, and ensure all the space available is fully utilised. Write your thoughts down and discuss with your assessor.

Questions

(See answer pointers at end of chapter.)
➤ **C1.3**: *2, 11* · · · · · · *7. A parent tells you she wants her daughter to keep her legs covered during PE* ◄ *sessions. How will you help this child to fully participate without going against her parent's wishes?*
➤ **C1.3**: *4* · · · · · · · *8. You have noticed that a sit-and-ride toy does not look quite right. It wobbles as* ◄ *the child scoots along on it. What action will you take?*
➤ **C1.3**: *5, 10, 13* · · · · *9. What are the health and safety requirements you need to be aware of before* ◄ *and during a physical exercise session?*

Record the questions and your full answers and share these with your assessor.

> **Did you know?**
> Children's physical development progresses rapidly during their first five years. An approximate guide to their potential adult height is to double their height on their second birthday.
>
> **C3.1**: 5

Extra ideas

➤ Encourage the children to dance by giving them ribbons to swish and twirl. · · · · **C1.3**: 3 ◄
Tie lengths of ribbon to thick bangles to wave.

➤ Using the 'Spider chart' photocopiable sheet on page 122, write 'Activities· · · · **C1.3**: 6, 7 ◄
involving gross motor skills' in the centre. Think of eight activities that could be
provided at your setting and write them in the surrounding boxes.

Element C1.4 Support children's quiet periods

➤ Your assessor can observe and question you. **C1.4**: Range 1c ◄

Making finger puppets
Number of children: six.

Resources
A4 thin card in different colours; sticky tape; felt-tipped pens; scissors; glue; scraps
of fabric; wool.

Preparation
Plan the activity using the 'Activity preparation' photocopiable sheet on page 121.
Ask your setting supervisor for support in doing this if necessary. Cut the card
into rectangles, approximately 6cm x 4cm.

What to do
➤ Make a finger puppet for yourself to show the children how it is made (see
illustration).
➤ Ask the children to draw an animal
or human face in the top middle
section of the long side of the card.
➤ Encourage the children to glue the
scraps of fabric and wool on the card as
hair and clothes.
➤ Invite the children to roll the card
into a tube that will fit on the end of
their fingers and fix with sticky tape.
➤ Encourage the children to tell each
other stories involving their characters.

Support and extension
Help young children with the cutting
and sticking. If they find it too difficult,
let them decorate with felt-tipped pens.

Tip

➤ Make sure you know which comforters belong to which child, and that they go home with them at the end of the day.

Do not expect a perfect finished product. The simplest finger puppets for very young children are to draw faces directly on to the finger ends with washable felt-tipped pens. Invite older children to make finger puppets from felt and sew the edges together.

Evaluation

Did the children have sufficient fine motor skills to do this activity? Was it, as planned, a quiet activity? If you do it again will you do it in the same way? If not what will you do differently and why? Were the children interested in using their puppets to tell a story to their friends?

Supporting activity

Think of the different ways you can use a range of puppets. Using the 'Spider chart' photocopiable sheet on page 122, write 'Puppets (type and use)' in the centre. In each surrounding box identify what type of puppet (finger puppet, hand puppet, marionette, large puppet, shadow puppet) you can use and how and why you can use it. Some ideas include language development, behaviour issues, story telling and multicultural awareness.

➤ **C1.4**: *1, 2, 3, 4, 5* · · ·

Case study

As part of the daily routine of your setting the period straight after lunch is designated a quiet period. Some children sleep on mats on the floor, others are provided with quiet activities in the book corner or at a table. Melody, however, becomes very upset every day when she realises it is rest time. Why do you think this happens and what can you do to reassure her? Write down the case study with your responses for your portfolio.

➤ **C1.4**: *2, 3* · · · · · · ·

Follow on

Make a chart showing the sleep requirements for children at different ages. Explain the importance of sleep.

Questions

(See answer pointers at end of chapter.)

➤ **C1.4**: *3* · · · · · · · · · **10.** *How can you ensure sleep and rest periods are consistent with the needs of the child and with patterns followed at home?*

➤ **C1.4**: *4* · · · · · · · · · **11.** *How can you ensure that a relaxed atmosphere is maintained during quiet*

➤ **C1.4**: *6* · · · · · · · · *periods?*

12. *What are the health and safety considerations you need to be aware of during rest periods?*

Record the questions and your full answers and share these with your assessor.

Did you know?

There are different cultural patterns and positions for sleeping. A young child used to sleeping with parents may have difficulty sleeping when placed alone in a cot.

Extra idea

Make a list of all the quiet activities that take place in your setting.

Practical ways of collecting evidence

Observe a child over a two-week period, noting when he or she is involved in quiet activity and when sleeping. See if there is a pattern to these episodes. Enquire if this meets with parent's expectations and preferences.

Check your progress

For this Unit you are expected to be observed by your assessor for at least one aspect of each range category for all four elements, although you can be observed for more if the opportunity arises. If some of the Performance Criteria are not observed you will need to collect evidence by some other means. This can be by an inspection of the setting in relationship to your role in the Elements covered, work products, reflective accounts, child observations, diaries, witness testimonies and projects.

Answer pointers

Ensure your answers are fully made for your assessor.

1. Access. Routine. Encouragement. Easily-removable clothes. Small toilets. Low washbasins. Clear instructions. Suitable potty. Teach how to flush the toilet.

2. Hygiene. Use and disposal of paper towels. Blowing noses. Privacy. Ownership of body. Respect for others.

3. Loose stools. Nappy rash. Offensive smell. Thread worms. Bruising.

4. Unhurried. Attractive food. Self service. Away from distractions. Right size furniture. With friends. Do not criticise. Encourage. Do not force. Set table.

5. Feeder beakers. Bibs. Plastic baby spoons. Non-slip plates. Small cutlery. High chairs. Aprons. Washable tables or covers.

6. Parents' wishes. Fingers. Chopsticks. Knife and fork. Sitting on floor.

7. Leggings. Change discretely. Treat normally. Be matter-of-fact. Answer children's questions. Do not draw attention to child.

8. Remove. Report to supervisor. Be observant. Identify damage.

9. Safety policies. Safety symbols on equipment. Check no hazards. Warm-up exercises. Non-slip. Carrying safely.

10. Talk to parents. Routine. Wake up. Alternatives to sleep. Minimise disturbances.

11. Minimise disturbances. Soft music. Routine. Quiet voices. Sing softly. Cuddles. Comforters.

12. Supervision. Policies and procedures. Intercom. Temperature. Ventilation. Hygiene. Toileting. Reduce cross-infection.

Further information

Early Years Care and Education NVQ Level 2: Student Handbook
Maria Robinson, Kate Beith and Lynda Pullan
(Heinemann, 1998)

C4 Support children's social and emotional development

This Unit focuses on the supporting role in the social and emotional development of children. It includes helping children to relate to others, to develop self-reliance and self-esteem, and to adjust to new settings. Aspects of behaviour are covered, such as recognising and dealing with feelings, and developing positive behaviour. It is applicable to all types of settings.

This chapter will enable you to:
C4.1 Help children to adjust to new settings
C4.2 Help children to relate to others
C4.3 Help children to develop self-reliance and self-esteem
C4.4 Help children to recognise and deal with their feelings
C4.5 Assist children to develop positive aspects of their behaviour.

Element C4.1 Help children to adjust to new settings

➤ **C4.1**: Range 1a, b, c, d, 2a, 3a

Your assessor can observe and question you. ◄

Settling in
Children need to know what is expected of them when they move to a new setting.
Number of children: appropriate to all children.

Preparation
Ensure you have discussed your role with your supervisor.

What to do
➤ Welcome the children with a smile, using the name the parent prefers to call their child.
➤ Introduce yourself and your colleagues.
➤ Show the children where to hang coats, put their bags or lunch boxes.
➤ Take the children to the toilet and help them if necessary. Ensure they wash their hands after, know where towels are and what they should do with used paper towels.
➤ Show the children around the setting.

early years
training & management

➤ Introduce the children to the activities and let them to have a go.
➤ Explain the need to wear aprons for messy activities in order to keep clothes clean. If willing, help the children put their aprons on. If they refuse, do not force them, but seek advice from colleagues.
➤ Talk to the children and listen to what they say.
➤ Let the children watch the others if they are not yet ready to join in.
➤ Introduce the children to each part of the routine as it happens. For instance at snack time show the children where to sit.
➤ Encourage the children to interact with others in the setting. If there are children in the setting who are familiar with the routine, pair them up with a new child.
➤ Help the children put their coats on at the end of the session.

Tip

➤ If the children are old enough, show them the clock face and indicate the time their parents will be coming back for them.
➤ Building a good relationship with a child from the start helps with the settling in process.

C4.1: 4, 6

Support and extension
Younger children may need cuddling and the use of distraction techniques. They may also have a comforter, such as a dummy or blanket. Older children may be more confident so encourage their independence without having unrealistic expectations.

Evaluation
How well did you deal with the new children settling in? Did you know what to do with distressed children? Can you think of other things that will help children to settle in? Did you discuss this with your supervisor?

Supporting activity
Encourage the children to draw a picture of their home and family to take home at the end of the day.

➤

Case study
It is the first full day Andrea has been in the setting and you have been asked to look after her. She is a bit bewildered and unsure of herself, and comes in clutching a small teddy. She has been to visit on two previous occasions, but this time her mum intends leaving after a few minutes. How will you welcome Andrea into the setting, introduce her to the activities and the everyday routine? Write down the case study with your responses for your portfolio.

C4.1: 1, 2, 3, 4, 5, 6, 7 ◄

Follow on
Make a list of ten skills children need to prepare for a move to a school setting. Identify areas such as putting on shoes and getting dressed.

Questions
(See answer pointers at end of chapter.)

➤ **1.** *In what ways can familiar items from home be used to help a child settle, in the*   **C4.1**: 2 ◄
early days of moving to a new setting?

➤ **2.** *How can you reassure a child who had not been left in a childcare or education* ·· **C4.1**: 5 ◄
setting before?

➤ **3.** *What are the strategies you can use to encourage children to join in the* ····· **C4.1**: 7 ◄
activities?

Record the questions and your full answers and share these with your assessor.

> **Did you know?**
> Children are individuals. Consequently they behave in different ways. Some children will settle down in a new setting very quickly, others will be distressed for some time. The role of the practitioner is to assess the child and respond according to need.

Extra ideas

➤ **C4.1**: 7 · · · · · · · · Using small world people, involve the children in a simple story about a day in the setting: 'All the children arrive in the mornings and hang their coats up on the pegs. They then sit on the carpet while their names are called. After that they play with the dough, the sand and the jigsaw puzzles. What do you think they make from the play dough? At break time they ...' ◄

➤ **C4.1**: 1 · · · · · · · · If it is the policy of the setting, make badges for the children with their names on. ◄

Element C4.2 Help children to relate to others

➤ **C4.2**: *Range 1a, b,* · · · Your assessor can observe and question you. ◄
2a, 3c

Ideas for circle time
Number of children: whole group.

Resources
Small soft toy; small bean bag.

Preparation
Discuss your role at circle time with your supervisor. You may be asked to collect the appropriate resources. Invite the children to sit in a circle.

What to do
➤ Explain the rules to the children before each game.
➤ Invite the children to play a passing game. Start the game by holding the toy and saying a sentence, such as

'My favourite story is ...',
'My favourite food is ...',
'I am really good at ....' or
'I am happy when...',

finishing the sentence with your answer. Pass the toy to the child nearest to you and invite them to say the same sentence, but adding their own ending. Accept and praise every statement without question. If a child does not want to say anything, let them pass the toy on and remain silent.
➤ Suggest playing a copying game to the children. Start a movement, such as clapping or nodding, and

encourage the rest of the group do the same. Change the movement and explain to the children that they have to watch and carefully change their movements too. Repeat the game using different movements.

➤ Invite the children to play 'Pass the smile'. Smile at the child nearest to you and encourage them to smile back at you. Explain that they should then turn to their neighbour and smile at them. Let the smile pass round the whole group until everyone is smiling!

➤ Challenge the children to play a memory game. Invite one child to stand in the centre of the circle and hold a small beanbag. Ask the child to call out the name of, and throw the beanbag to, another child. Ask the children to try and remember whose names have been called, and choose someone who has not had a turn. Make sure everyone gets a turn.

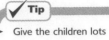
> Give the children lots of opportunities to work co-operatively with their peers.

Support and extension
Circle time can be adapted to accommodate all ages and abilities. Keep games simple for the younger children and add more complex tasks or rules with older children.

Evaluation
You will not be expected to lead the whole group for circle time, but did you join in and support and encourage the children at their level? Did the activity encourage children to relate to one another? Can you think of other activities that can be included at circle time?

Supporting activities
Practise the activities with pairs of children or in threes or fours, rather than the whole group. Encourage the children to communicate with others, helping when they can.

➤ ### Case study
Ben is a quiet, shy child, often seen playing on his own. His Grandmother is concerned that he does not seem to be making friends. What can you do to help him make friends and join in activities with the other children in the class? Write down the case study with your responses for your portfolio.

C4.2: 1, 2, 6 ◄

➤ ### Follow on
Think of the games and activities that help children relate to others. Collect notes about them in a notebook and add to the list as you learn more. Make notes against each one when you think of new variations.

C4.2: 1, 6 ◄

Questions
(See answer pointers at end of chapter.)

➤ **4.** *How can you help children to work co-operatively with others, and what* · · · · · **C4.2**: 1 ◄
opportunities are there to do so in the daily routine?

➤ **5.** *How can you encourage children to interact with others so they can learn to* · · · **C4.2**: 6 ◄
understand and respect children and adults from various backgrounds?

➤ **6.** *Can you give examples of anti-social behaviour and describe how you can deal* · · **C4.2**: 7 ◄
with the incidents?

Record the questions and your full answers and share these with your assessor.

Did you know?
In her book, *Children First* (Random House, 2000), Penelope Leach states, 'Children like to learn because they want to know – everything there is to know about their world – and they rather particularly want to know how to behave because they want to be like their parents or parent figures and to have their approval'.

Extra idea
Caring for pets is one way for a child to take responsibility and gain respect for others. Talk to the children about the needs of animals, what to feed them, their shelter and how they live. Encourage the children to feed pets in the setting.

Element C4.3 Help children to develop self-reliance and self esteem

 C4.3: *Range 1a, b,* · · · · *2a, b, c*

Your assessor can observe and question you.

Clothes shop
Number of children: four.

Resources
Table; chairs; screen; clothes rail; coat hangers; storage boxes; variety of costumes from different cultures; hats; handbags; other accessories; cash register; play money; writing pad; pencils; telephone; carrier bags; full length mirror; strips of cardboard; thick felt-tipped pen; Blu-tack.

Preparation
Plan the activity using the 'Activity preparation' photocopiable sheet on page 121. Ask your setting supervisor for support in doing this if necessary. Help set up the imaginative play area.

What to do
➤ Help to arrange the furniture in the imaginative play area to create a clothes shop and hang all the costumes on the coat hangers.
➤ Sort the hats, scarves, shawls and bags into the storage boxes.
➤ Place the cash register with money, telephone, pad and pen on the 'counter' table.
➤ Write out labels identifying the different aspects of the shop, such as 'hatbox' and 'handbags', and fix in the appropriate places.
➤ Ask the children to guess what you have set up.
➤ Let the children choose a name for the clothes shop. Write the shop name on card and fix to the screen.
➤ Share the money out so the 'customers' can come into the shop to spend it.
➤ Encourage the children to choose outfits

and to try on and buy the items.

➤ Help the children where necessary, but let them try to put the garments on, do up the fastenings and admire themselves in the mirror.

➤ Praise the children for their independence.

➤ Encourage the children to try on costumes from cultures different to their own, and try not to stereotype. For example, it is acceptable for boys to wear shawls and skirts.

➤ Encourage the children to express themselves through the costumes.

✓ **Tip**

➤ Value the languages the children bring to the setting to boost self-esteem.

C4.3: 6

Support and extension

Ensure the outfits are simple enough for young children to put on by themselves. Let older children try fastening buttons, ties and belts on their own. Encourage older children to write out receipts or shopping lists, and to ring up suppliers on the telephone.

Evaluation

Were the costumes easy for the children to put on and take off? Did the children work co-operatively by helping one another? Could you stand back a little to allow them to choose for themselves and try things on without help? Was conversation stimulated? What other things could you have done?

Supporting activity

Collect pictures of people from around the world wearing different sorts of costumes. Make a display using the pictures as well as real costumes. Ask the children to bring in photographs of themselves and their families wearing traditional costumes or their favourite outfit.

➤ ### Case study

Micah has only been in this country for a few months, having fled with his family from a war zone. He is settling down, although you have not heard him speak yet. The setting is used to working with asylum seekers and has lots of toys and equipment to help them settle. There is also a high staff:child ratio. How can you help Micah feel secure and able to build his self-esteem after such a traumatic start? Write down the case study with your responses for your portfolio.

C4.3: 3, 6, 7, 8, 9 ◄

Follow on

If you want to find out about asylum seekers and refugee children visit the websites for the Refugee Council: **www.refugeecouncil.org.uk**; Save the Children: **www.savethechildren.org.uk** and the United Nations: **www.unitednations.org.uk**.

Questions

(See answer pointers at end of chapter.)

➤ **7.** *What decisions are children able to make for themselves in the setting, and · · · ·* **C4.3**: 1, 2 ◄
what is your role in relation to them communicating their needs?

➤ **8.** *What self-help skills can be practised as part of the regular routine and how can* · · **C4.3**: 4, 5 ◄
you encourage the children to develop them?

➤ **9.** *What is meant by the term stereotypical?* · · · · · · · · · · · · · · · · · **C4.3**: 8 ◄

Record the questions and your full answers and share these with your assessor.

Did you know?
'Successful personal, social and emotional development is critical for very young children in all aspects of their lives and gives them the best opportunity for success in all other areas of learning.' *Curriculum Guidance for the Foundation Stage* (DfEE, 2000)

Extra ideas

➤ **C4.3**: 3 · · · · · · · · ➤ Keep a checklist during one session and tick off each time you give a child a chance to make a decision, such as a choice of paint colour, biscuit or to stay inside or go outdoors. ◄

➤ **C4.3**: 3, 4· · · · · · · ➤ Using the 'Spider chart' photocopiable sheet on page 122, place 'Self-esteem' ◄ in the centre and in the surrounding boxes write eight different ways of helping children to gain confidence and self-reliance in the daily routine.

Element C4.4 Help children to recognise and deal with their feelings

➤ **C4.4**: *Range 1a, b,* · · Your assessor can observe and question you. ◄
c, 2a, b, 3a, b, c, d

Puppet play
Number of children: four.

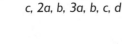

➤ Children may be frustrated because English is not their first language and they cannot express themselves. Give them extra attention, simple instructions and lots of encouragement.

C4.4: 3

Resources
Selection of glove puppets; large grocery carton; paint: PVA glue; brushes; aprons; table covering; aprons.

Preparation
Plan the activity using the 'Activity preparation' photocopiable sheet on page 121. Ask your setting supervisor for support in doing this if necessary. With great care, cut a hole out of the two opposite sides of the cardboard carton, big enough for a child's hand to fit through while holding a puppet. Cut a section out of the cardboard box to make the front of a puppet theatre (see illustration). Protect the table with a washable cover. Mix one part PVA glue to three parts paint, adding a drop of water if it is too thick to paint with.

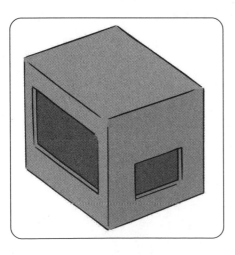

What to do
➤ Help the children to put on their aprons.
➤ Ask the children to paint the outside of the box until it is fully covered and leave to dry.
➤ Help the children to wash the paint from their hands.
➤ Show the children the puppets and explain that when the puppet theatre is dry they will be able to act out little plays.
➤ Encourage the children to use the puppets to act out their feelings. Seek advice from your supervisor if you are unsure how to do this.
➤ Give scenarios, such as one puppet is sad and the other tries to make him happy, one puppet is bullying another and he tells him to stop it or one puppet is frightened of the dark and another comforts her. Children may want to talk through other situations.

➤ Keep the situations simple and let the children take turns to be the different characters.

Support and extension

Younger children will enjoy painting the puppet theatre. You may need to prompt the children with their stories and help them to think through the situation. Once the older children have started these scenes they will come up with their own suggestions for using puppets to raise other issues.

Evaluation

Were you able to prepare the activity with minimal support? Did you feel confident in working with the children? Having done it once, do you feel you can encourage the children to act out issues around behaviour using puppets on another occasion?

Supporting activities

Make yourself some notes on situations you can suggest to children to act out. Copy the glove puppet outline (see illustration) and help the children to make their own puppets. Use felt to prevent fraying. Introduce different types of puppets, such as gluing a face from a magazine to a strip of card wrapped around the end of a finger and fixed with sticky tape, string puppets or faces drawn on the ends of your fingers.

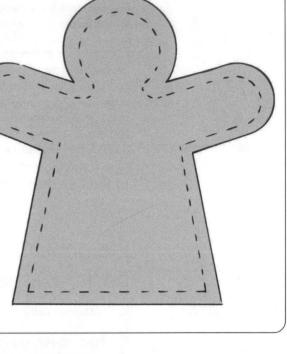

➤ **Case study**

With a new baby in the house, Selina, at two years and four months, has reacted by having regular temper tantrums. She stamps her feet, screams and throws herself to the floor. Afterwards she is quite distressed and comes to you for comfort. How can you help Selina deal with her feelings and reassure her? Write down the case study with your responses for your portfolio.

C4.4: 4, 7 ◄

Follow on

Make a list of six things that may affect children's behaviour, beginning with a new baby. Consider how you can help them overcome any difficulties and discuss with your assessor.

Questions

(See answer pointers at end of chapter.)

➤ **10.** *What examples of positive and negative feelings can you identify? List at least* · · **C4.4**: 1, 2, 3, 5 ◄
five of each.

➤ **11.** *What activities can you suggest where children can learn to identify and deal* · · **C4.4**: 1, 3 ◄
with their own and others' feelings?

➤ **12.** *If there is concern about a child's recognition and expression of feelings, who* · · **C4.4**: 6 ◄
can you expect this to be discussed with?

Record the questions and your full answers and share these with your assessor.

Did you know?

Toddler tantrums are a normal part of development. They become much less frequent by the end of the child's third year. Be positive, through tantrums children are learning important lessons about themselves.

Extra ideas

➤ Older children can be helped to deal with their feelings through dance and movement. Encourage the children to act out bad feelings in pairs, for example one stamps in front of another, and the other jumps back. Repeat the sequence and invite the two children to swap their actions. Afterwards ask them to smile at one another and shake hands. Let the children work out their own sequence of actions and reactions.

➤ Use a mirror to show individual children how their faces can show different feelings, including happy, sad and angry.

Element C4.5 Assist children to develop positive aspects of their behaviour

➤ **C4.5**: Range 1a, b, 2a, b, c, d

Your assessor can observe and question you.

Behaviour game

You may play this game in its simple form with younger children by yourself. If the intention is to use the game to raise behavioural issues you may wish to have an experienced practitioner playing with you. Set the ground rules of game playing with the children before you start playing it.
Number of children: two or four.

Resources

'Behaviour game' photocopiable sheet on page 123; two or four counters; dice.

Preparation

Discuss the appropriate activity with your supervisor in the setting, following simple rules for younger children and more complex ones for older children. Enlarge the 'Behaviour game' sheet to A3 size. This activity can be cross-referenced to **M1**.

What to do

➤ Game one.
  ♦ Start the game with the counters on the circle at the Start.
  ♦ Ask the children in turn to throw the dice and move their counters around the board in a clockwise direction.
  ♦ Read the action word on the circle that the counter lands on, such as bullying or caring, and ask the child if it is a good or bad thing.
  ♦ Continue until all the circles have been landed on at least once.

➤ Game two.
    ♦ Follow the rules for Game one, but if a six is thrown slide the counter
    along the straight line to another circle instead of counting along the circles.
    ♦ Discuss the words as before.
➤ Game three.
    ♦ Use the same rules as Game one and Game two but make the game more
    challenging by asking the children to give examples of the action word.

Support and extension

➤ Keep the game very simple for young children, reading the words to them and
travelling around the board twice. Invite older children to read the words for
themselves and travel around the board four times. Emphasise the positive
aspects of behaviour. Develop the game with discussion on behavioural issues.
Ask questions, such as 'What would you do if you were being bullied?', 'How can
you make friends?' and 'When should you take turns?'.

Cross-reference to **C8** ◀

Evaluation

Were you able to enlarge the photocopiable sheet satisfactorily? Did the children
stick to the rules you had given them? Did the children suggest any alternative
rules? If so can you put them into practice next time you play the game? Did you
feel confident in playing a game about positive and negative behaviour? What
more do you feel you need to learn about dealing with behaviour?

✔ **Tip**

➤ Praise achievements no
matter how small.

C4.5: 2

➤ 'Pay maximum attention
to appropriate behaviour and
minimum attention to
inappropriate behaviour.'
Gerard Gordon, *Managing
Challenging Children* (Prim-Ed
Publishing, 1996)

C4.5: 4

Supporting activity

Notice how many times the children show positive behaviour and give them
praise.

Case study

➤ Dean has a reputation for bad behaviour, so when he moves to your setting
you expect the worst. Surprisingly you find the expected bad behaviour does
not happen. What can you do to ensure this happy state continues and
recognise Dean's positive behaviour? Write down the case study with your
responses for your portfolio.

C4.5: 2   ◀

Follow on

➤ Temper tantrums in a child are often started by a particular action that
triggers them. This can be having a toy taken from them by another child,
wanting a toy another child is playing with or being frustrated because of not
having the skills to do a task. Observe a child who has tantrums to see if you
can identify if there is a particular reason for them. Then consider how you
can reduce the temper tantrums until the child grows out of them.

C4.5: 4, 6, 7, 8   ◀

Questions

(See answer pointers at end of chapter.)

➤ **13.** *By providing activities and experiences, boredom and frustration can be* · · · · ·   **C4.5**: 1   ◀
minimised. How can you ensure that what is offered will do this?

➤ **14.** *What are the goals and boundaries that should be set to ensure the physical* · ·   **C4.5**: 3   ◀
and emotional well-being of the children in the setting?

➤ **15.** *What are the sanctions that can be applied when unacceptable behaviour is* · ·   **C4.5**: 5   ◀
identified?

Record the questions and your full answers and share these with your assessor.

Did you know?

Every setting will have a behaviour policy. Make yourself familiar with yours.

Extra idea

➤ **C4.5**: 6 · · · · · · · · · Use reward systems for reinforcing positive behaviour, such as reward charts with ◄
stars, ink stampers on squared paper or marbles in a jar (transfer one to a
personalised jar with the child's name on each time positive behaviour is noticed).

Practical ways of collecting evidence

Keep a diary for a few days. Record positive and negative behaviour of children
you observe in the setting. State briefly who was involved (use an initial or code,
do not record information to identify the children), what the behaviour was, how
it was resolved and any contributing causes. Photocopy a page as evidence for
your portfolio.

Check your progress

You are expected to be directly observed for at least one aspect of each
Range category for all five elements in this unit, although you may be
observed for more aspects if the opportunity arises. Some of the
Performance Criteria and aspects of Range statements may not be observed
by your assessor and you can collect evidence for these by several other
means. Select at least two other methods of evidence collection from
reflective accounts of your work, work products, diaries, activity plans and
preparation sheets, child observations, questioning on policies and feedback
from parents.

Answer pointers

Ensure your answers are fully made for your assessor.

1. Bring a teddy. Interest table. Cardboard boxes for craft modelling. Old
greetings cards. Comforters. Photograph.

2. Give attention. Be available. Involve in activities. Reassure parent will be back.
Parent can leave an item they have to come back for – show child.

3. Watch others. Encourage to join in. Make it exciting. Give choice. Make it
familiar. Go at child's pace.

4. Group games. Table-top games. Setting out equipment. Clearing away. Turn
taking. Dinner queue. Helping one another.

5. Anti-racist. Projects. Bring things in from home. Do not dismiss. Invite
community visitors in. Multicultural play.

6. Results in physical pain. Destroys property. Insults. Hurts feelings. Change
behaviour. Praise the positive. Reassure.

7. Choosing activities. Choosing food. Choosing books. Role-play. Selecting
songs. Choosing the story. Being given a choice of craft materials. Listen.
Encourage. Action. Using ideas and suggestions. Selecting toys.

8. Shoes. Coats. Eating. Dressing and undressing. Toileting. Hand washing. Praise.
Notice. Tell colleagues. Share with others.

9. Putting people in boxes. Making assumptions about people with disabilities.
Racial assumptions. Gender restrictions.

10. Anger. Frustration. Happiness. Achievement. Jealousy. Pride.
11. Puppets. Story telling. Circle time. Imaginative play. Dolls.
12. Supervisor. Parents. Colleagues. Other professionals.
13. Appropriate developmental level. Attractive. Interesting. Varied. Achievable.
14. Helping one another. Turn taking. Co-operating. Doing as asked. Kindness.
15. Withdrawal of privileges. Removal from activity.

Further information

Children First
Penelope Leach
(Random House, 2000)

Curriculum Guidance for the Foundation Stage
(DfEE, 2000)

My First Book of the World
Janet Allison Brown
(Brimax Books, 2001)

Personal, Social and Emotional Development
Jean Evans
Around the Year series
(Scholastic, 2001)

Personal, Social and Emotional Development
Barbara J Leach
Goals for the Foundation Stage series
(Scholastic, 2003)

C8 Implement planned activities for sensory and intellectual development

This Unit covers a variety of activities typical of those provided in care and education settings. It includes creative play, games, cooking, manipulative play and examining interesting objects.

This chapter will enable you to:
C8.1 Provide activities, equipment and materials for creative play
C8.2 Play games with children
C8.3 Assist children with cooking activities
C8.4 Provide opportunities and equipment for manipulative play
C8.5 Examine objects of interest with children.

Element C8.1 Provide activities, equipment and materials for creative play

➤ **C8.1**: Range: 1c, 2a, b, 3a, b, 4b

·Your assessor can observe and question you. ◄

Painting for pleasure
Number of children: four.

Resources
Ready-mixed paint in a variety of colours; assorted brushes; pots and dishes; paper; assorted equipment as appropriate; aprons; protective covering.

Preparation
Plan the activity using the 'Activity preparation' photocopiable sheet on page 121. Ask your setting supervisor for support in doing this if necessary. Preparation will vary according to the activity chosen. Ensure everything is ready for the children at the stage you wish them to join in, for example, if they are to start painting the paint should be put in containers.

What to do
➤ Offer different coloured paints and paper and allow the children to paint whatever they want. Do not guide them, make suggestions or help them to do it.
➤ Let the children experiment with mixing the colours.
➤ Make potato prints by cutting a shape into half a potato. Paint over the surface of the potato, press on to the paper and lift off carefully.
➤ Mix paint with washing-up liquid in a tub and show the

children how to blow through a straw to produce bubbles. Ensure the children do not suck through the straws! Place paper over the bubbles to produce a print.

➤ Cut out a butterfly shape from paper and fold in half. Invite the children to paint on one half, fold the second half over and gently press down to produce a symmetrical pattern.

➤ Spread paint directly on to a washable surface. Let the children finger-paint patterns in the paint and press a sheet of paper on the design to take a print.

➤ Help the children draw a picture on a sheet of paper with a wax candle. Paint over the page and watch the picture magically appear.

➤ Place flat leaves on paper. Ask the children to paint over the leaves and then remove them to leave a reverse leaf print on the page.

Support and extension

Young children may suck rather than blow down the straws so this may not be an appropriate activity. An adult should use a sharp knife to cut potato prints. Invite older children to make their own printing blocks from objects glued to a block of wood.

Evaluation

Did the activity interest the children? Was it pitched at the right level? Did you use appropriate coverings to keep the children and equipment clean? How did you manage to prevent the spread of paint? Were the children able to express themselves creatively in this medium?

Supporting activity

➤ Take the children on a walk to collect materials for use in a creative activity. · · · · · **C8.1**: 6
Look for fir cones, leaves, sticks, acorns, conkers, stones and shells. Use these to make a garden on a plate. Alternatively, make a garden in the sand tray, glue one to a box or make a collage.

Case study

➤ Brooke has not yet gained the skills needed to cut and stick. He gets   **C8.1**: 1, 6
frustrated and, after trying for a few minutes, throws the scissors down and goes to do something else. How can you encourage Brooke to gain the necessary skills? What alternative creative activities can you suggest until he is able to fully participate? Write down the case study with your responses for your portfolio.

Follow on

➤ Make a chart showing physical development at different stages. Indicate   **C8.1**: 1
when children can be expected to reach major milestones and to have gained skills you can notice in the regular routine and activities in the setting.

Questions

(See answer pointers at end of chapter.)

➤ **1.** *Can you suggest alternatives to sand play, and how would you offer them?* · · · · **C8.1**: 1 ◄

➤ **2.** *What health and safety checks need to be made before doing creative activities?* **C8.1**: 3, 4, 5 ◄

➤ **3.** *Protective coverings and clothes are required for messy activities. What do you* · · **C8.1**: 7, 8 ◄
expect to be available in the setting?

Record the questions and your full answers and share these with your assessor.

➤ Provide children with the relevant materials and give assistance where necessary, but let them create their own finished product.

C8.1: 1

➤ Collect all sorts of brushes to use with paint, such as sterilised toothbrushes, household paint brushes, scrubbing brushes, nailbrushes, fine brushes, thick brushes, flat brushes and rounded brushes.

Did you know?

When children first start drawing and painting, the movement comes from the shoulder. As they develop it becomes more controlled and the movement is from the elbow. Later, hand movements are used. The last skill to develop is the pincer grip movement, which is required to hold a pencil and make small actions to produce a mark.

Extra idea

➤ **C8.1**: *1, 2, 6* · · · · · Collect cardboard cartons, cereal boxes, tubes and food containers for craft modelling. Let the children cut, stick, glue them together and paint them. ◄

Element C8.2 Play games with children

➤ **C8.2**: *Range 1a, b,* · · · Your assessor can observe and question you. ◄
c, d, e, f, 2a, b, c,
3a, b

Hop frog hop
Number of children: four.

Resources
'Hop frog hop' photocopiable sheet on page 124; scissors; dice.

Preparation
Enlarge the 'Hop frog hop' sheet to A3 size. Laminate the sheet to extend the life of the game. Cut out the four frog counters and glue them on to thin card. Fold along the line to make them stand up. If appropriate, the children can to do this themselves.

What to do
➤ Invite the children to sit around a table with the frog game.
➤ Explain the rules of the game to the children.
➤ Take turns to throw the dice.
➤ Start in the middle of the pond and jump the frog from lily pad to lily pad according to the number thrown on the dice.
➤ When landing on a lily pad with a flower, jump on two more lily pads.
➤ The first frog to land on the last lily pad catches the bug and wins the game.

Support and extension
Use a die showing ones and twos with young children. You can make this by placing labels over the spots on a traditional die. Invite older children to colour in the frog counters or make their own from Plasticine. The lily pads can be coloured green and the background pond blue.

➤ Give clear instructions to children when playing games.

Evaluation
Did you enlarge the photocopiable sheet satisfactorily? Were you able to explain the rules of the game to the children? Did the children take turns? What did the children learn from this game? Can you suggest new rules for playing this game? Will you play this game again?

Supporting activities

➤ Sing the counting rhyme 'Five Little Speckled Frogs' (Traditional). Look up frogs in a non-fiction book. Suggest taking the children on a walk to a pond. Discuss with your supervisor.

*Cross-reference to **C9**, **M1*** ◄

Case study

➤ Eden loves to play games, but as he has learning difficulties he finds it hard to follow the rules. He wants it to be his turn all the time and forgets that other children are playing. In what ways can you help him to understand that part of the enjoyment is playing with other people and to understand the rules? Write down the case study with your responses for your portfolio.

***C8.2**: 1, 2, 3, 4, 5, 6, 7, 8, 9, 10* ◄

Follow on

➤ Find out if your setting has a policy on only encouraging non-competitive games. Does this mean children can never win a game? Talk this over with your supervisor and record your findings in your portfolio.

***C8.2**: 8* ◄

Questions

(See answer pointers at end of chapter.)

➤ **4.** *What are the health and safety considerations you need to make when selecting and playing games?* · · · · · · ***C8.2**: 2, cross-reference to **E2*** ◄

➤ **5.** *Can you give examples of non-competitive games that you can play with the children outdoors?* · · · · · ***C8.2**: 8* ◄

➤ **6.** *In what ways can you encourage children to play games that are fair for all?* · · · ***C8.2**: 10* ◄

Record the questions and your full answers and share these with your assessor.

Did you know?
Familiar games like 'Ludo' and 'Snakes and ladders' have their origins in India.

Extra idea

➤ Categorise all the games played in your setting under the headings table top games, listening games and games without equipment. Place in your portfolio. · · · ***C8.2**: Range 1a, d, f* ◄

Element C8.3 Assist children with cooking activities

➤ Your assessor can observe and question you. · ***C8.3**: Range 1b, 2b* ◄

Cheese animals
Number of children: four.

Resources
200g self-raising flour; 50g cooking fat; 80g Cheddar cheese; one cherry tomato; water; flour; four small bowls; four small wooden spoons; four small rolling pins, or two to share; baking sheet; jug; animal-shaped pastry cutters; palette knife; aprons; anti-bacterial spray; clean cloth or paper towels.

✔ **Tip**

➤ A cookery activity does not have to involve heat. There are many no-bake recipes you can use with young children.

Preparation

Plan the activity using the 'Activity preparation' photocopiable sheet on page 121. Ask your setting supervisor for support in doing this if necessary. Wash your hands, put on an apron and clean the table top with the anti-bacterial spray. Collect the ingredients and utensils for the chosen recipe. Grate the cheese and cut the tomato into tiny pieces. Ask for permission from parents and carers to taste foods and check for any food allergies or dietary requirements. Pre-heat the oven to 400°F/200°C/Gas Mark 6. Supervise the children as they wash their hands and put on their aprons.

What to do

➤ Give each child a bowl.
➤ Divide the flour and fat equally between the children and show them how to rub the fat in, to resemble breadcrumbs.
➤ Give each child a quarter of the cheese to mix in.
➤ Add enough water for the children to make a stiff dough.
➤ Flour the table top and invite the children to roll the dough out to approximately 4cm thick.
➤ Let the children cut out animal shapes with the pastry cutters and place a small piece of tomato on, to represent an eye.
➤ Slide the animals shapes on to a baking sheet with the palette knife and bake for ten minutes or until golden brown. For safety reasons an adult should put the baking sheet in and take it out of the oven.
➤ Let the pastry cool before removing from the baking sheet and sharing as a group.

Support and extension

Give younger children additional help where required, particularly when rubbing the fat into the flour and cutting out the animals. Older children will be able to manage the process and may be able to grate the cheese with supervision.

Evaluation

➤ Cross-reference to **E2**

Did the activity go well? Did you feel you were in control of the situation? Did you feel able to supervise all the children during the activity? Were you able to give relevant assistance to the children and any other adults? What can you do to improve the activity? Could you make cheese animals on another occasion? If not why not?

Supporting activity

Try some other recipes with the children. See the 'Easy recipes' photocopiable sheet on page 125 for more ideas.

➤ **C8.3**: 1, 2, 11, 12

Case study

You are working with children of different ages, all of whom like cooking. You are planning a cookery session where everyone can join in. How can you organise the session so the competence of the oldest child is used and the little ones feel they are joining in? Write down the case study with your responses for your portfolio.

> ## Follow on
> Make a collection of recipes, including some from different cultures. Add notes when you have tried them to say how they worked, what you will change or tips for next time.

C8.3: 1, 8, 11 ◄

Questions
(See answer pointers at end of chapter.)

➤ **7.** *Can you describe how to prepare, store and use ingredients for cooking and* · · · **C8.3**: 6 ◄
cooked food safely and hygienically?

➤ **8.** *How can you actively include aspects of different cultures in a cookery activity?* · · **C8.3**: 8 ◄

➤ **9.** *In what ways can you extend children's learning and enjoyment through cooking?* **C8.3**: 10 ◄

Record the questions and your full answers and share these with your assessor.

> ### Did you know?
> The temperature of ovens varies a little from one to another. If you are going to use an unfamiliar oven it is best to test, or ask others, if it heats to a higher or lower temperature than the recipes states. All temperatures given in recipes are for guidance only.

Oven temperature guidance

Degrees Fahrenheit	Degrees Centigrade	Gas Mark	Description
275	130	1	Very cool
300	150	2	Cool
325	165	3	Warm
350	180	4	Moderate
375	190	5	Moderate to hot
400	200	6	Fairly hot
425	220	7	Hot
450	230	8	Hot
475	245	9	Very hot

Extra ideas

➤ **C8.3**: *1, 2, 3, 4, 5,* · · ·   ➤ For a winter activity make some bird cake with the children. Melt some meat
9, 10, 12, cross-   dripping or hard fat with great care. Give the children wild bird food and kitchen
reference to **C8.5**   scraps, such as stale cake, breadcrumbs, breakfast cereal and chopped bacon rind, ◄
to mix together in a bowl. When the fat has cooled, but not set, pour over the
mixture, stir and pack firmly into washed yoghurt pots. Leave to set in the fridge
and then put outside on the bird table.

➤ **C8.3**: *1, 2, 10, 11* · · ·   ➤ Preserve edible flowers and leaves, using only those known not to be
poisonous. Choose from rose petals, parsley leaves, violets, nasturtium flowers ◄
and mint leaves. Wipe the leaves and petals gently with a tissue before painting
with egg white. Sprinkle individually to coat with caster sugar. Place on a waxed
sheet in a baking tray. Leave on the lowest heat in the oven for several hours, or
overnight, with the oven door half open, to dry out. Use as cake decorations.

Element C8.4 Provide opportunities and equipment for manipulative play

➤ **C8.4**: *Range 2a, b* · · ·   Your assessor can observe and question you. ◄

Play dough

Play dough is a satisfying medium for all ages. There are different recipes to try at
different times. Some are suitable for model making, others for rolling and
squeezing and some for baking and keeping. Through this medium children gain
hand-eye co-ordination, develop their sense of touch and sight, increase their
concentration and their understanding of length, weight, shape, size and
thickness. It encourages creativity and manipulation. Try some of the play dough
activities and optional presentations made below.
Number of children: four.

Resources

'Play dough recipes' photocopiable sheet on page 126;
ingredients according to recipe.

Preparation

Plan the activity using the 'Activity preparation'
photocopiable sheet on page 121. Ask your setting
supervisor for support in doing this if necessary. Prepare the
play dough beforehand and keep it in a plastic box in the
fridge until required.

What to do

➤ Give each child a portion of dough, either in one colour
or smaller amounts in two or more colours.
➤ Add glitter to the play dough.
➤ On some occasions give the children the play dough
without any implements and encourage them to experience its
texture and smell, to manipulate it and to be creative with it.
➤ Use the 'Spongy dough' recipe for pounding, poking,
kneading, squeezing and pinching.

➤ Use the 'Two-way play dough' or the 'Long-lasting play dough' recipes for making models and making impressions in the dough with fingers and hard objects, such as keys or pieces of Duplo.

➤ Offer a variety of implements, including plastic cutlery, rolling pins, patty tins and biscuit cutters.

➤ On other occasions let the children choose from a selection of tea strainers, potato mashers, large old keys, ice-lolly sticks and corks.

➤ Offer plates, blunt knives and paper cake cases for imaginative meal making.

➤ Add food flavourings, such as peppermint or strawberry to stimulate the children's senses.

Tip

➤ Cutting out simple shapes, such as animal shapes, can make great sewing cards. Punch holes around the edge with a hole-punch and let the children thread wool through. Stiffen the ends of the wool with nail varnish.

Support and extension

Ensure the children do not put the play dough in their mouths, particularly if using heavily-salted dough. Encourage older children to make the play dough themselves. Take the children through the recipe step by step, giving them plenty of time. If baking the 'Two-way play dough', attach small pieces of dough before putting in the oven with a little water. Once baked the dough will be very hard and will last indefinitely, unless dropped many times. Finish the models off by painting and varnishing with diluted PVA glue. Food for the home corner can be made in this way.

Evaluation

Observe the children using the play dough. Did you see them manipulating the material? Did they use their imagination? Where they creative? Did they gain lots of experience of handling the dough in different ways? Did they copy one another? Did the activity stimulate language development? Were the children using fine motor skills, such as finger and thumb pincer movements?

Supporting activity

Using the 'Spider chart' photocopiable sheet on page 122, write 'Play dough' in the centre. In as many of the surrounding boxes as you can, write the different learning experiences the children have gained from this activity. Place this in your portfolio and cross-reference into the relevant Units.

➤ **Case study**
You have noticed that Mollie has some difficulty in fitting toys together. You have discussed it with your supervisor and she has suggested you give extra time to Mollie to help to develop these skills. How will you set about this? How do you propose to extend the opportunities for developing hand-eye co-ordination over a period of time? Write down the case study with your responses for your portfolio.

C8.4: *1, 4, 6, 10* ◄

➤ **Follow on**
Suggest ways in which a parent can encourage a child to develop manipulative skills in the home.

C8.4: *4* ◄

Questions
(See answer pointers at end of chapter.)

➤ **10.** *Under what circumstances is it appropriate to offer woodworking tools and* · · · · **C8.4**: *1* ◄
materials in the setting?

➤ **11.** *What do you need to think about when setting out large construction* · · · · · · **C8.4**: *1, 2, 3, 5* ◄
equipment to ensure a satisfactory play experience for the children?

➤ **C8.4**: 8, 9, 10, · · · · ·
cross-reference to
E2

12. *What are the health and safety issues you need to consider when offering small-scale construction toys?* ◄

Record the questions and your full answers and share these with your assessor.

> **Did you know?** ❓
> Fitting jigsaw puzzles together enables a child to recognise shapes and manipulate them into place. Both of these skills help with reading and writing later on. Before being able to recognise letters children need to be able to recognise shapes. To hold a pencil requires the skills of picking up and gripping.

Extra idea
Make a list of all the opportunities for manipulative play in your setting. Categorise them under the headings: small-scale construction, large-scale construction, puzzles and shape fitting, gross motor skills and fine manipulative skills, to cover the range. Place the list in your portfolio.

Element C8.5 Examine objects of interest with children

Having an interest theme and themed experiences helps both adults and children to focus on the objects. In discussion with your supervisor suggest a 'Colour' theme day.

➤ **C8.5**: *range 1a, b, c,* · ·
d, e, 2a, b, 3a, b, c,
d, e

Your assessor can observe and question you. ◄

Today is orange
There are lots of 'Colour' themed activities you can do in the setting. A selection is given here. Discuss the theme with the children and listen to their views.
Number of children: all children can be involved in different aspects.

Resources
Interest table with display board behind; plain material to cover table that shows up orange, such as green or dark blue; orange objects for display; orange flowers; orange play dough; orange paint plus one other colour; sheets of coloured sugar paper, including orange; orange crêpe paper; glue; scissors; coloured pens; thin card; orange icing; biscuits; blunt knife; oranges and tangerines; carrots.

Preparation
Plan various activities using the 'Activity preparation' photocopiable sheet on page 121. Ask your setting supervisor for support in doing this if necessary. Set up an interest table with a cover. Before your 'orange day' ask the children to bring in orange objects from home.

What to do
➤ Suggest that the children collect as many orange objects as they can from around the setting.
➤ Involve the children in setting up an instant display on the interest table.
➤ Offer the children shades of orange paint and another colour, such as brown,

and ask them to study the orange objects and paint them on paper.

➤ Mount the children's paintings on orange paper and display them on the board behind the interest table.

➤ Peel an orange and share the segments out at snack time.

➤ Invite the children to draw and colour-in some oranges and a basket. Help the children cut out the shapes they have drawn, arrange the oranges in the basket and glue them on to some card.

➤ Bring in some orange flowers, such as marigolds, to put on the interest table.

➤ Make orange play dough for the children.

➤ Add orange crêpe paper to the water tray and invite the children to watch the water change colour.

➤ Show the children how to use orange icing to ice some biscuits for snack time.

➤ Ask the children to scrub some carrots to eat at snack time.

➤ As a group talk about all the orange items and their qualities.

Support and extension
Choose activities suitable for the developmental level of the children. Let older children mix their own shades of orange from red and yellow paint.

Evaluation
How many spontaneous ideas came out of this activity? Can you think of other activities you can do for a different 'Colour' themed day? Were the children interested in the orange theme? Did you have any surprises?

Supporting activity
Let the children have a paint-mixing session. Offer the children the range of primary colours (red, yellow and blue) and challenge them to make as many different colours they can from them. Remember red and yellow makes orange, red and blue makes purple, and yellow and blue makes green. Adding black or white extends the range of shades.

Case study
➤ Chahandni brings in an old birds' nest from his garden. Your supervisor suggests you think of ways of using it to stimulate play and learning. How will you use this item of interest? What activities can you suggest that will develop the children's skills and knowledge, using the nest as a stimulus? Write down the case study with your responses for your portfolio.

C8.5: 1, 2, 3, 4, 5, 6, ◄
7, 8

Follow on
➤ Find out about the health and safety aspects of using materials such as birds' nests and plant materials. Consider the health and safety aspects involved in feeding the birds and making bird cake.

C8.5: 8, cross-reference ◄
to **C8.3**, **E2**

✔ **Tip**

➤ When presenting, displaying or discussing objects of interest remember to include cultural aspects different to your own.

C8.5: 2

➤ Provide a magnifying glass to help children examine interesting objects.

C8.5: 6

Questions
(See answer pointers at end of chapter.)

➤ **C8.5**: 5, 6, 8 . . . . **13.** *When planning to examine objects of interest, such as the birds' nest, what are* ◄ *the considerations you need to make to ensure they are accessible and attractive to the children, as well as safe?*

➤ **C8.5**: 7 . . . . **14.** *When examining objects of interest, which senses do you expect the children to* ◄ *use? Give examples for each sense.*

➤ **C8.5**: 8 . . . . **15.** *How can you ensure toddlers can enjoy objects of interest in a safe manner?* ◄

Record the questions and your full answers and share these with your assessor.

Did you know?
Children find the world fascinating. Sometimes adults need to look through the eyes of the child to appreciate the wonders all around.

Extra idea
➤ **C8.5**: 5 . . . . Ask the children and practitioners to bring in an object that is very special to ◄ them. Give the children the opportunity, perhaps in a quiet corner, to tell you about their object.

Practical ways of collecting evidence
Keep a notebook in your pocket to record the activities you do with the children over a period of time. Ensure you have collected evidence of at least one activity, preferably more, relating to each of the five Elements in this Unit: creative, games, cooking, manipulative play and objects of interest.

Check your progress
For this Unit you are expected to implement activities that support intellectual and sensory development. Your assessor will directly observe you for at least one aspect of each of the Range statements for all five Elements. Some of the Performance Criteria may not be observed and you are expected to collect evidence for this by other means. This can be by reflective accounts of your own practice, work products, such as home-made games and photographs, log books, plans, child observations, case studies, inspection of the setting, for instance the cookery area, and witness testimonies by colleagues who have seen you work.

Answer pointers

Ensure your answers are fully made for your assessor.

1. Coconut fibre. Salt. Dried beans, peas and lentils. Sieved sawdust. Sand tray. Table-top tray. Plastic sheet on floor. Baking tray.

2. Safety. Allergies. Non-toxic. Not dangerous. Suitable positioning. Not damaged.

3. Keep children clean. Protect environment and furniture. Table covering. Floor covering. Aprons. Newspapers. Hats. Paper towels.

4. Age of children. Small pieces. Clean. Follow manufacturer's instructions. Safe environment. Non-toxic.

5. Parachute games. Ring games. 'Hokey cokey'. 'Follow the leader'. 'Ring-o-ring-o-roses'.

6. Explain the rules. Turn taking. Appropriate games for developmental level. Ensure everyone gets a chance to play. Let both boys and girls have equal chances.

7. Wash hands. Fridge. Use-by date. Clean surfaces. Wear clean aprons. Clean environment. Cover. Supervise. Suitable utensils.

8. Ingredients. Cooking vessels. Methods. Presentation. Recipes.

9. Weighing. Counting. Writing out recipe. Shopping. Changes to ingredients. New words. Knowledge and understanding.

10. Age appropriate. Under supervision. Following instruction. Due regard to health and safety policies.

11. Away from bikes. Contained area. Checked for safety. Appropriate to age group. Controlled group. Big enough area. Not too close to other activities.

12. Check before use. Clean. Remove damaged items. Away from babies. Supervised.

13. Children's level. Attractive. Can touch them. Non-toxic. Stimulating. Promotes language development.

14. Sight. Hearing. Touch. Smell. Sometimes taste.

15. Supervision. No small pieces. In a glass fronted cupboard to observe. In a lidded fish tank for all round vision. Safe objects. Cannot be swallowed.

Further information

Multicultural Activities
Carole Court
Early Years Activity Chest series
(Scholastic, 2000)

C9 Implement planned activities for the development of language and communication skills

This Unit covers working with children in ways that support their learning and development through music, role-play, stories, books, rhymes and activities that aid talking and listening. You are expected to be able to select and implement activities within the curriculum plan, both indoors and in outdoor play space. You will also need to be aware of the relevant health and safety considerations and any adaptations to be made for children with special needs.

This chapter will enable you to:
C9.1 Implement music sessions
C9.2 Implement and participate in talking and listening activities
C9.3 Select and use equipment and materials to stimulate role-play
C9.4 Select and display books
C9.5 Relate stories and rhymes.

Element C9.1 Implement music sessions

➤ **C9.1**: Range 1a, b, c, d, 2b, 3a, b, d

Your assessor can observe and question you. ◄

Musical story
Number of children: small group.

Resources
Musical story, such as the 'A walk in the woods' photocopiable sheet on page 127; assorted musical instruments for each child.

Preparation
Plan the activity using the 'Activity preparation' photocopiable sheet on page 121. Ask your setting supervisor for support in doing this if necessary. Identify an area, away from the other children, that is suitable for story telling, with a carpet or ring of chairs to sit on.

What to do
➤ Invite the children to sit down and explain that you are going to tell them a story with sounds.
➤ Show the children the instruments.
➤ Tell the children the sort of sounds you need to find instruments for and let them select which

instruments should be used for which sounds.
➤ Practise making the sounds as a group.
➤ Tell the children a very simple story, such as 'A walk in the woods'. Read the story first so the children know what to expect.
➤ On the second telling, bring in the instrument sounds, indicating to the individual children when it is their turn to come in. Give the children plenty of time to make their sound.
➤ Repeat the story several times as the children gain confidence in their part.

Support and extension

Keep the story simple for younger children by only using two or three instruments. Challenge older children to make their own instruments, finishing them by painting and varnishing with diluted PVA glue.

Evaluation

Did you feel confident telling the story? Could you have made it better? Were you able to control the children, so they made their sound at the right time? Will you make up your own story next time? What do you think the children gained from this activity?

Supporting activities

Sing 'I am the Music Man' (Traditional), miming the actions of the song. Make musical instruments with the older children, or make some yourself for the younger children. Make shakers from a variety of containers with tight fitting lids. Make simple rattles from a variety of beads, bobbins and macaroni, threaded on to a shoelace and knotted to form a circle.

✔ **Tip**

➤ Do not neglect traditional songs and nursery rhymes.

C9.1: 1

➤ Sing nursery songs in languages other than English.

C9.1: 2, 4

Rather than playing music all the time, use it constructively. Offer a variety of types of music and music from different cultures. Then when it is played on tape or disc children are more likely to notice it.

C9.1: 4

Case study

➤ Fourteen-month old Jaina loves music. As soon as she hears any she stops what she is doing, sways and turns round and round in circles. How many different ways can you think of to develop this enjoyment further? Write down the case study with your responses for your portfolio.

C9.1: 1, 2, 3, 4, 5, 6, 7 ◄

Follow on

➤ Music gives the opportunity to introduce different cultural experiences. Find out what music and musical instruments you have from different cultures in your setting. See if you can borrow some from parents or a local multicultural resource centre. Cut out pictures of multi-cultural instruments from catalogues, stick on cards and share with the children. Talk to the children about the differences and similarities, and encourage them to share their personal experiences.

C9.1: 4 ◄

Questions

(See answer pointers at end of chapter.)
➤ **1.** *A number of aspects of learning can be gained from songs and action rhymes. Can you identify the benefits and give examples?*   **C9.1**: 1, 2 ◄

➤ **2.** *How can you engage the children's attention in order to encourage them to participate in music and singing?*   **C9.1**: 5 ◄

➤ **3.** *What are the musical instruments and visual aids you can use for the following ages: a) seven years, b) four years, c) six months?*   **C9.1**: 6 ◄

Record the questions and your full answers and share these with your assessor.

Did you know?

Research indicates that music played to the infant before birth and in the early months stimulates the brain. (*Baby Wisdom* by Deborah Jackson, Hodder & Stoughton, 2002)

➤ C9.1: *5* · · · · · · ·

Extra ideas

Encourage the use of the body in music sessions. Suggest that children become actively involved in the music by using their bodies to represent the sounds. For example, ask them to slap their thighs, stamp their feet, click their fingers and clap their hands in response to the music. ◄

Element C9.2 Implement and participate in talking and listening activities

➤ C9.2: *Range 1a, b,* · ·
2b 3a, b

Your assessor can observe and question you. ◄

Harvest plate

Number of children: six.

Resources

Paper plates, selection from dried peas, beans, lentils, pumpkin seeds, sesame seeds, rice, pasta, corn and breakfast cereals; margarine pots; PVA glue; glue spreaders.

Preparation

Plan the activity using the 'Activity preparation' photocopiable sheet on page 121. Ask your setting supervisor for support in doing this if necessary. Set out the seeds, pulses and cereals in individual containers.

✔ Tip

➤ Communication starts at birth. Talk to an infant right from the earliest days.

What to do

➤ Talk to the children about sowing seeds, the growing and ripening of crops and the gathering of the harvest. Explain that this happens all over the world.
➤ Ask the children to identify their favourite foods. Talk about food in different cultures.
➤ As a group, look at the foodstuffs you have provided. Help the children to describe the qualities of the cereals and pulses. Identify colours (green, orange, white and brown) and descriptions (smooth, rough, wrinkly, small and tiny).
➤ Describe the shapes of the cereals and pulses (round, spherical, long, short).
➤ Talk about the texture and touch of the materials. Ask what sort of sound they make when they are touched.
➤ Discuss the methods of using and cooking the foodstuffs you have provided.
➤ Give the children a paper plate each to make their own harvest plate. Discuss how they can arrange the foodstuffs on the plates. It can be in clusters, in patterns, a random scattering or a combination. Encourage the children to glue the materials to the plate.

Support and extension

Keep the conversation within the developmental level of the children. Supervise young children to ensure they do not eat the foodstuffs or push them in their ears or up their noses. Provide non-fiction books on harvest for older children. Alternatives to gluing cereals and pulses include cutting food pictures from magazines, or cutting out paper or fabric food, to glue on the plate.

Evaluation

Did the activity stimulate discussion? Were you able to encourage the children to extend and reinforce their language and communication? Were you well prepared to answer the questions of the children? Do you need to find out more about harvests around the world and food processing? Did the children enjoy the activity?

Supporting activity

Place small seeds in a tube, with the ends well sealed, to turn from end to end to make rain shakers. Discuss the weather and rain sounds. Sing 'I hear Thunder' (Traditional). Find out about harvest festivals around the world.

Case study

You know that Louis hears and understands what you are saying by his reactions. If you ask if he wants a drink he runs to the cupboard where the cups are kept. If you offer him a piece of apple he holds out his hand. He will not, however, talk to anyone outside the home. What ways can you suggest to encourage him to speak? Write down the case study with your responses for your portfolio.

C9.2: 2, 4, 6, 7, 8 ◄

Follow on

Make a note of the talking, listening and joining-in games you know. Include 'I spy with my little eye, something that is ... green ... a circle ... smooth ...' and circle games where children have to listen to previous contributions, such as 'I went to the shops and I bought ... a bunch of carrots, some milk and a sack of potatoes'. Ask a colleague for a witness testimony to confirm you have played these games with the children.

C9.2: 1, 2, 5 ◄

Questions

(See answer pointers at end of chapter.)

► **4.** *How can you identify a child with communication difficulties and how can you* · · · **C9.2**: 5 ◄
adapt the activities to accommodate their needs?

► **5.** *What form of visual and tactile aids can you suggest to engage the children's* · · · **C9.2**: 6 ◄
attention and aid their communication?

► **6.** *Can you identify the opportunities in the daily routine in your setting that* · · · · · **C9.2**: 7 ◄
positively encourage children to talk to adults?

Record the questions and your full answers and share these with your assessor.

Did you know?

There are approximately 5000 languages spoken in the world today. Bilingualism, or multilingualism, is a natural way of life for hundreds of millions of people. Children who are able to communicate in more than one language have an added advantage over those who only speak one language. As they have additional words to use to express themselves and different grammatical structures, they often have the ability to think more flexibly and creatively.

Extra ideas

➤ **C9.2**: 2 · · · · · · · ·   ➤ Use a tape recorder so children can record their own voices and play it back. ◄

➤ **C9.2**: 6 · · · · · · · ·   ➤ Draw faces on the ends of your fingers with felt-tipped pens and use them to ◄ 'talk' to the children.

Element C9.3 Select and use equipment and materials to stimulate role-play

➤ **C9.3**: Range 1a, 2a, · · ·   Your assessor can observe and question you.   ◄
3a

The café

Number of children: four.

Resources

Small tables; chairs; tablecloths; vases of flowers; plastic cutlery; crockery; plastic food; baskets; dishes; pad; pens; waiter and waitress aprons; dressing-up clothes for café customers, including bags and purses; cash register; toy money; several copies of 'Menu' photocopiable sheet on page 128.

Preparation

Plan the activity using the 'Activity preparation' photocopiable sheet on page 121. Ask your setting supervisor for support in doing this if necessary. Mount one or more copies of the menu on stand-up cards for the counter. Cut out individual labels, stick to a folded piece of card and stand by the relevant food. Stick one menu per table on to card for the customers to use. If desired, laminate the menus to lengthen their life. Set out the imaginative play area as a café. Put the food on the counter and group the chairs around small tables with tablecloths and flowers on. Make and fix a large café sign near the entrance.

What to do

➤ Talk to the children about what happens in a café.

➤ Ask if any of the children have been to a café and discuss their experiences.

➤ Show the children the menu. Read out the list and add in their suggestion of prices.

➤ Let the children choose which roles they will play, including waiter or waitress, customer, server and cashier.

➤ Offer the children clothes to wear for the appropriate roles.

➤ Encourage the waiter or waitress to greet customers, show them the range of food, show them to their seats and write their order on the pad.

➤ Suggest that the waiter or waitress collects the food from the server and takes it to the customer.

➤ Encourage the customer to choose from the menu, pretend to consume the food and go to pay the cashier.

➤ Encourage the children to make their own decisions and to play all the roles. Once the children know the roles and routine allow them to operate the café as they want to.

Support and extension

Younger children will operate in a simpler form. Let them take the role-play at their own pace. They do not have to be waiters or waitresses, but can operate on a self-service basis. Challenge older children to work out the cost of purchases and change. Older children can make hats or hatbands for the waiters and waitresses, paper flowers for the table, the large café sign and their own menus.

Evaluation

Were you able to find all the resources you needed for this activity? Did you add any not listed above? Did the children come up with any innovations you had not expected? If you present this activity again will you include these extra ideas? Did the role-play stimulate language and communication? What did you learn from presenting the role-play and watching the children play?

Supporting activity

Make 'Two-way play dough' from the 'Play dough recipes' photocopiable sheet on page 126 and mould into food shapes. Bake until hard, paint and varnish with diluted PVA glue. Make food from scrap materials. Triangles of sponge, with a felt-tipped line drawn around the side can represent sandwiches. Fruit moulded from papier-mâché and painted can be presented in a fruit bowl. Boxes covered in white paper and decorated with Plasticine 'cherries' can be a cake. Make, bake and serve real food. Change the café into a Chinese Takeaway.

Case study

➤ Your supervisor has given you the responsibility of setting up the imaginative play area. You decide to talk to the children first to see what interests them at the moment. Carys has recently been in hospital and tells you about it. The other children join in with their experiences and you say you will set up a hospital so the children can act it out. What items will you put in the hospital and how will you encourage the children to use the area? Write down the case study with your responses for your portfolio.

C9.3: 1, 2, 5, 6   ◄

Follow on

➤ Listen to the children talking about their experiences. This may give you ideas for future role-play areas. Note down any thoughts and how they may be implemented. Discuss with your colleagues and supervisor and share your ideas with your assessor.

C9.3: 3, 5, 6   ◄

✔ **Tip**

➤ Provide newspapers in different languages to add an authentic touch to role-play in the home corner.

C9.3: 6, 7

➤ On fine days set up the role-play area outside.

C9.3: 2

➤ Try to offer a range of dressing-up clothes from different cultures.

C9.3: 6, 7

Questions
(See answer pointers at end of chapter.)

➤ **C9.3**: 1 · · · · · · ·

7. *Can you list six different ideas for setting up the imaginative play area for role-play? Indicate what items you can provide for each role-play.* ◄

➤ **C9.3**: 2, 4, cross- · · · ·
reference to **E2**

8. *What are the health and safety issues concerning the materials and equipment provided for role-play?* ◄

➤ **C9.3**: 3 · · · · · · · ·

9. *What resources can you provide for child-led role-play, where the children can make their own decisions on the form of the play?* ◄

Record the questions and your full answers and share these with your assessor.

Did you know?
'... Children encouraged to initiate their own play were better at reading and writing by the time they reached primary school...'
Professor Kathy Sylva, Educational Psychologist, Oxford University.

➤ **C9.3**: 6, 7 · · · · · · ·

Extra idea ◄
When setting up the home corner, alternate between a Western home, an Asian home, a Chinese home and an African home.

Element C9.4 Select and display books

➤ **C9.4**: Range 1a, b, · · ·
c, d, 2a, 3a, b, c, d

Your assessor can observe and question you. ◄

Book display
Number of children: for all children.

Resources
Table; selected books; plain sheet; small strong cardboard cartons; small toys and objects to match theme of books.

What to do
➤ Ensure the table for the display is in an area where it is unlikely to be knocked, with comfortable seating close by.
➤ In discussion with your supervisor, choose a theme for the display, such as myself, animals, the weather, other lands or festivals.
➤ For a general display, choose both fiction and non-fiction books on the theme, within the developmental range of the children.
➤ Look for bright attractive books.
➤ Choose the illustrations with care. Do they show different styles, photographs and drawings, positive multicultural images, are non-stereotypical, and show people wearing glasses and with disabilities?
➤ Books may have words or only show

pictures. Perhaps you could include examples of both. Include some dual language texts.

➤ Ensure all books are in good condition, removing any defective ones for repair.

➤ Choose small toys or artefacts that go with the theme, such as animals from the farm set for an animal theme, or religious artefacts for a festival theme.

➤ Arrange the small cardboard boxes strategically on the table, with the sheet thrown over the boxes and table. Arrange the books and objects on and between the boxes to make an attractive arrangement.

➤ Encourage the children to visit the display, to look at and handle the books and to talk about them.

➤ Read the books to the children.

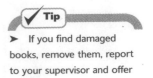

Tip

➤ If you find damaged books, remove them, report to your supervisor and offer to repair them.

C9.4: 7

Support and extension

Ensure books are suitable for the ages and abilities of the children. Provide young children with fewer and stronger books with more pictures than words. Challenge older children with books with more text, more choice and more reference books. All will need carefully chosen illustrations as described above.

Evaluation

Was this a useful exercise for you? Did you have any difficulty in identifying suitable books? Did you find any dual language books?

Supporting activity

Use your local library. Find out if they lend books to early years settings and, if so, how many and for how long? Look to see what sort of children's books they have in stock? Do they fulfil the requirements of text, illustrations, and attractiveness that you have been looking for? If your library does not loan to settings, you may want to borrow the maximum number on your own membership ticket to share with the children.

➤ **Case study**

Will loves books. You notice he is a bit rough with them and they are sometimes torn. You have seen him stacking them up and climbing on them, using them as tunnels with his cars, as well as eagerly pinching the pages in order to turn them over. How can you help Will to continue to enjoy books while at the same time learning to respect them and use them properly? Write down the case study with your responses for your portfolio.

C9.4: 7, 8 ◄

➤ **Follow on**

Check the correct way to store books to ensure the safety of children and staff. Talk to your supervisor about different ways of placing, positioning and storing books in your setting.

C9.4: 8, cross-reference ◄ to **E2**

Questions

(See answer pointers at end of chapter.)

➤ **10.** *Can you list ten themes you can use for a book display in your setting?* · · · · · · **C9.4**: 1 ◄

➤ **11.** *In what ways can you ensure that the surroundings are comfortable for* · · · · · **C9.4**: 2 ◄
children to look at books?

➤ **12.** *What does it mean to have positive images of people of various backgrounds* · · **C9.4**: 4 ◄
and experiences?

Record the questions and your full answers and share these with your assessor.

Did you know?

Children do not acquire reading skills at the same time. The experience of words on a page needs to be built up and the love of books established at an early age.

Extra ideas

➤ **C9.4**: *1, 4* . . . . . .

➤ If there is a display rack in your setting set up a display there, using the same criteria as described above. ◄

➤ **C9.4**: *5* . . . .

➤ Make a list of the different types of books, such as story books, situational books and reference books. Give examples from each category. ◄

Element C9.5 Relate stories and rhymes

➤ **C9.5**: *Range 1a, b, c, d, 2b, c, 3a, b, c, d, 4a, b, c*

Your assessor can observe and question you. ◄

Story aids

Number of children: two or three children, or a larger group.

Resources

Story book; assorted equipment as appropriate to activity.

Preparation

Plan the activity using the 'Activity preparation' photocopiable sheet on page 121. Ask your setting supervisor for support in doing this if necessary. Read the story through beforehand to familiarise yourself with it. Collect or prepare the relevant story aids. You may wish to use the 'Story aids' photocopiable sheet on page 129.

What to do

➤ Use a felt board and felt shapes that will adhere to the board and can be moved about accordingly as you tell the story.
➤ Cut out paper figures or objects and stick a piece of felt on the back. Use with a felt board to relate the story.
➤ Enlarge and photocopy the 'Story aids' sheet. Colour in, cut out and stick a piece of sandpaper to the back of the images. Use these to tell the story with a felt board.

➤ Use a magnetic board and shapes.

➤ Use 3-D objects to illustrate a story, such as a teddy bear or a wooden train.

➤ Use puppets to attract the children's attention and aid concentration.

➤ Dress up as the main character in a story or the narrator. Hats and shawls are very useful.

➤ Use musical instruments to represent the sounds in the story.

➤ Use your body as a story aid, clapping and waving your hands, stamping your feet, nodding your head and dancing.

➤ Use finger puppets. These are small enough to keep in your pocket until you need them.

➤ Put story-related objects in a box or bag and remove one by one as they appear in the story.

➤ Talk about the pictures in the story book.

Tip

➤ Use multi-lingual tapes of rhymes and stories to share with the children.

Support and extension
Ensure the story is appropriate for the developmental level of the children. The younger the children the more valuable the story aids will be in attracting their attention.

Evaluation
If you have used visual aids for story telling, do you feel those chosen were the best ones on this occasion? Can you suggest alternatives if you tell the same story at some time in the future? Can you think of any other types of visual aids? Did you tell the story with confidence? Can you do it any better?

Supporting activity
If you are artistic you may be able to draw your own visual aids. Use all your skills and talents for the benefit of the children.

Case study
➤ You work in a setting that has children from several different cultural backgrounds. Amahri feels a bit insecure, as he has moved several times in his short life. He does not communicate well but loves listening to a story and joining in with the rhymes. Building on this positive aspect of behaviour, how can you help him, and the other children in the setting, through rhymes and story telling? Write down the case study with your responses for your portfolio.

C9.5: 1, 2, 3, 5, 6, 7 ◄

Follow on
Make a collection of rhymes. If you do not know any rhymes in languages other than English, ask a colleague or parent to tape-record some for you, with the translation.

Questions
(See answer pointers at end of chapter.)

➤ **13.** *What do you think the children are gaining through the sharing of rhymes?* · · · **C9.5**: 1, 2, 6 ◄

➤ **14.** *Can you describe the various methods of delivering a story, giving the* · · · · · **C9.5**: 3 ◄
advantages of each technique.

➤ **15.** *How can you ensure children's comments and reactions are handled in such* · · · **C9.5**: 4, 8, 9 ◄
a way as to develop positive aspects of behaviour?

Record the questions and your full answers and share these with your assessor.

Did you know?
The nursery rhyme 'Baa, Baa, Black Sheep' (Traditional) has survived for 600 years, and refers to the wool trade of the 14th or 15th century.

Extra idea

➤ **C9.4**: 7 · · · · · · · · · Use the opportunity of the children sitting down for a snack to have a rhyme time. Let the children choose familiar rhymes and you help them out as the accompaniment.

Practical ways of collecting evidence
Tape record your music, story-telling and rhyme sessions and put the tape in your portfolio.

Check your progress
You are expected to be directly observed by your assessor, under real working conditions, to cover at least one aspect of each Range statement in each of the five Elements. You may be observed for more than one aspect, but if not you can provide evidence by other means. Other forms of evidence are from inspection of the setting to see a book display, reflective accounts, work products like visual aids, diary pages, preparation sheets, child observation and assignments.

Answer pointers
Ensure your answers are fully made for your assessor.
1. Counting. Literacy – rhyming words, new words. Social development. Language and communication. Cultural differences. 'One, Two, Three, Four, Five, Once I Caught a Fish Alive', 'Here We Go Round the Mulberry Bush' (both Traditional).
2. Actions – clapping. Facial expressions – smiling. Singing instead of talking. Eye contact. Playing an instrument. Use of music. Imagination.
3. Children make own instruments. Simple safe instruments. Bought instruments. Posters. Books. Bells on socks.
4. Hearing impaired. Non-speakers. Lack confidence. Not fluent speakers. Speech impairment. Look at child. Face unobstructed. Clear instructions. Light in front of you.
5. Puppets. Telephone. Objects of interest. Tactile activities. Weather board.
6. Talking during toileting. News time. Circle time. During activities. Lunch time. Snack time.
7. Home corner. Hospital. Dentist. Travel Agent. Big chair. Stethoscope. Telephone. Stainless steel cooking pots. Chopsticks. Holiday brochures. White coats. Ethnically-diverse dolls. Pad and pen. Bed or mattress. Instruments.
8. Safe access. Clean. Checked. Damaged items removed. Repaired. Hats fumigated. Safe.
9. Dressing-up clothes. Curtains. Cardboard boxes. Dolls. Seats. Hats. Cardboard-box television. Net curtains. Sheet.
10. Home life. Holidays. Jobs people do. Nature. Stories from different cultures.
11. Carpet. Bean bags. Sofa. Stools. Homely. Attractive.
12. Girls as leaders. Black people in authority. Disabled people taking active

roles. Girls in sport. Men in caring roles. Women doing DIY.

13. Rhyming words. New words. Repetition. Security. Comfort. Enjoyment. Tradition. Sharing.

14. Reading. Visual aids. Without visual aids. Memory. Actions. Without actions. Attract attention. Prompt. Need familiar story. Can use unfamiliar story. Maintain eye contact.

15. Maintain self-confidence. Personalise stories. Settle children. Comfortable area.

Further information

Supporting Language and Literacy:
A Handbook for Those Who Assist in Early Years Settings
Suzi Clipson-Boyles
(David Fulton Publishers, 1996)

Developing Bilingualism in Children
Welsh Language Board
www.welsh-language-board.org.uk

E1 Maintain an attractive, stimulating and reassuring environment for children

This Unit emphasises the importance of maintaining an attractive, stimulating and reassuring physical environment, including displays. It includes living areas, play areas and both indoors and outdoors. This Unit is appropriate for workers in all types of settings where children are cared for individually or in groups.
This chapter will enable you to:

E1.1 Maintain the physical environment
E1.2 Prepare and maintain displays
E1.3 Maintain a reassuring environment.

Element E1.1 Maintain the physical environment

➤ *E1.1: Range 1a, b, c, d*

Your assessor can observe and question you. ◄

Know your setting
In order to maintain the physical environment in a safe and satisfactory manner, it is necessary to know what is there, what makes it safe and your role in the maintenance of the setting.

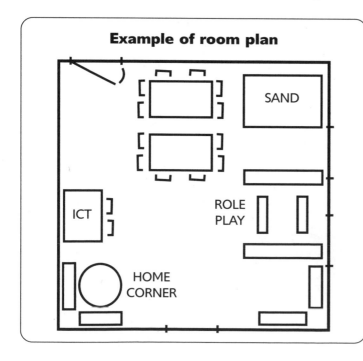

Example of room plan

(SAND, ICT, ROLE PLAY, HOME CORNER)

Resources
'Setting checklist' photocopiable sheet on page 130.

What to do
➤ Draw a plan of your setting showing the layout of the room(s).
➤ Indicate where the main pieces of furniture are situated.
➤ Show where the activities are placed. You may need to copy your original plan to show the different sessions.
➤ Mark where the fire exits are.
➤ Complete the 'Setting checklist' sheet. There is additional space for you to add areas that relate particularly to your setting.
➤ As you complete the checklist, check your responses with your supervisor.
➤ Share the checklist with your assessor and put in your portfolio.

➤ Draw a plan of the outdoor area, indicating the location of fixed furniture and play equipment.
➤ Describe the garden areas and grass and show gates and safety equipment.
➤ Indicate sections where particular activities take place.
➤ Place in your portfolio.

✓ **Tip**

➤ Tidy up as you go. Toys and other objects left in the wrong place can cause accidents.

Support and extension

If you see something you are unsure about check with your supervisor why it is there.

Evaluation

Did you learn something new from undertaking this task? Ask yourself questions as you go round the setting. Can you make suggestions for a different layout? Give your reasons for this. Did you observe any safety aspects that concerned you? Share these with your supervisor and assessor.

Supporting activities

Using the 'Spider chart' photocopiable sheet on page 122, write 'Children with disabilities' in the centre. Consider your setting and how the physical environment accommodates children with different sorts of disabilities. Write different aspects in the surrounding boxes. Include access to rooms and activities, access to the toilet and adaptations. Ask your supervisor if you can try a new layout in the setting. This can be a small area, indoors or out. Give reasons why you are making this suggestion. Write a reflective account, saying what you have done, whether it worked satisfactorily and what the feedback was from children and colleagues. Discuss your role with your supervisor. Make notes during the meeting and include in your portfolio.

Case study

➤ Daniella attends your setting. She has a visual impairment and the supervisor has delegated you to check the setting, to make sure the environment is suitable for her needs. How can you help her make the most of her opportunities? What are the aspects you need to consider for a child with this particular condition? Write down the case study with your responses for your portfolio.

E1.1: 2, 3, 6 ◀

Follow on

➤ Consider the need for a safe environment for children with other disabilities. Are they different than for the rest of the children? Think about hearing impairment, mobility impairment, challenging behaviour and wheelchair users.

E1.1: 1 ◀

Questions

(See answer pointers at end of chapter.)

➤ **1.** *When selecting and arranging furniture (tables, chairs, storage), what factors do you need to consider that makes them suitable for childcare and early years settings?*
E1.1: 3 ◀

➤ **2.** *In what ways can children be positively encouraged to take on responsibilities in the setting?*
E1.1: 6 ◀

➤ **3.** *Why may you want to make changes to the layout of the setting?* · · · · · · · ·
E1.1: 7 ◀

Record the questions and your full answers and share these with your assessor.

Did you know?
Each year 15000 children are born with disabilities.

Extra idea

➤ **E1.1**: *2, 3* . . . . . . ◄ If possible, arrange to have a look around another setting . Look at the similarities ◄ and differences to your regular setting. If you see some good ideas share these with your assessor.

Element E1.2 Prepare and maintain displays

➤ **E1.2**: *Range 1a, b,* . . · *c, 2a, b, c, d*   Your assessor can observe your display and question you.   ◄

Setting up displays
Number of children: all children can be involved.

Resources
Display boards and tables; board covering; sheet or sari; board stapler; drawing pins; Blu-Tack; scissors; glue stick; thick felt-tipped pens; card; ribbon or string; display items.

Preparation
Ask your supervisor to agree any displays you plan and prepare. You may be responsible for a display board or a particular aspect as part of the team. Gather the background and display materials before setting up the display.

What to do
➤ In consultation with colleagues, select a theme.
➤ Involve the children in ways appropriate to the display.
➤ Decide on the type of presentation. Is it to be on a board, a table, a table with a board behind it, a screen or hanging from the ceiling?
➤ Prepare the surface by covering the board with coloured paper to show up the articles to be attached.
➤ Cover a table with a plain sheet or a sari. The surface can be made more interesting if small boxes are fixed beneath the sheet to raise different areas or to have something to lean objects against.
➤ Consider the material to be displayed. Children's drawings can look more effective if mounted first on contrasting paper. Glue on to paper that is slightly larger than the original. Cut out according to the shape of the picture, whether it is to be a rectangular border or shaped to follow the lines of the drawing.
➤ Display a mixture of children's work and posters, magazine pictures and postcards.
➤ Arrange on the board in an interesting and effective way. Not all pictures need to be fixed flat – stapling the two edges closer together, with the middle of the paper projecting forward, can be very effective.
➤ Label to identify the artist or illustration. Use the script favoured by the setting.
➤ Curl any printing or painting done by babies into a tube, attach ribbons and hang from the ceiling.

✔ **Tip**

➤ Ensure you spell children's names correctly.

E1.2: *3*

➤ Use community languages on your headings and labels.

E1.2: *4*

➤ Make sure work from all the children is included in displays, even though the quality of the finished product may be variable.

E1.2: *8*

➤ Keep the children and parents interested by frequently changing the display.

E1.2: *9*

➤ Be extra careful with displays in baby rooms. Ensure they are safe, with no small parts to swallow.

E1.2: *10*

➤ Set up a 3-D display on the table. Ensure it is non-poisonous and safe.
➤ Displays can also be fixed to windows and doors.

Support and extension

Involve the children at their level of development. Ensure they have appropriate materials, for example skin-tone paper and paints for self-portraits. Remember, the process of producing the picture is more important than the finished product.

Evaluation

Did you adhere to all safety procedures in putting the display up? Check the visual appeal of the display. Is it symmetrical or deliberately non-symmetrical? Does the colour scheme work? Is the mounting satisfactory? Are the labels you have used big and bold enough? Are the children proud of their work?

Supporting activities

Suggestions for displays include: festivals; ourselves; fairy tales; food; homes; celebrations; around the world; colours; numbers; water.

➤ **Case study**

Four-year-old Jennifer wants to be a soldier when she grows up. She acts the part, tries to get the other children to march and dresses up in army fatigues. Her father is in the army, as are many of the parents of the other children in the setting. There are plans to make an army display. What can you put in this display and how will you present it? Write down the case study with your responses for your portfolio.

E1.2: 1, 2, 3, 6, 7 ◄

➤ **Follow on**

When you put up displays consider the images you are presenting. Ask yourself if they show positive images, including boys caring for others, girls being doctors, black people in leadership roles and disabled people playing a full part in society.

E1.2: 3 ◄

Questions

(See answer pointers at end of chapter.)

➤ **4.** *In what ways are learning opportunities provided for children through displays?* · · **E1.2**: 1 ◄

➤ **5.** *When displaying natural materials, what considerations should be made to* · · · · **E1.3**: 5 ◄
ensure the children's health and safety?

➤ **6.** *How can children and their parents be actively involved in the selection of* · · · · **E1.2**: 6, cross- ◄
materials in displays? reference to **P1**

Record the questions and your full answers and share these with your assessor.

Extra idea

➤ **E1.2**: 1 · · · · · · · · Be inventive with displays. Display pictures on a huge cardboard box or fix to the ◄ walls of the home corner and call it a gallery.

Element E1.3 Maintain a reassuring environment

➤ **E1.3**: Range 1b, 2a, · · Your assessor can observe and question you. ◄
b, c, d

Quiet time round robin

Children do not want to be active all the time. They also need quiet times to recuperate. Having a routine that offers both active and quiet play, giving individual attention and providing familiar activities, such as cutting, sticking and round robins, is reassuring to the children.
Number of children: six.

Resources

Firm card for pattern; coloured background card; brown card (or white card and brown felt-tipped pens); red tissue paper; small amounts of orange card; two 80cm lengths of thin orange ribbon per child; small pair goggle eyes; PVA glue; double-sided sticky-backed small foam pads (often used to attach posters); 'Round robin' photocopiable sheet on page 131.

Preparation

Plan the activity using the 'Activity preparation' photocopiable sheet on page 121. Ask your setting supervisor for support in doing this if necessary. Make cardboard templates of the robin's body, breast and feet using the 'Round robin' sheet.

What to do

➤ Show the children the picture of the robin and explain that they will be their own robins.
➤ Ask the children to draw around the body template on to the brown card.
➤ Place the red breast template on top of the body to show where it fits. Draw a line to show the separation.
➤ Help the children cut out the whole body shape.
➤ Invite the children to tear the tissue paper into small pieces, roll it into balls and stick on the breast area.
➤ Help the children to cut a triangular beak and two feet from the orange card.
➤ Let the children glue on the beak and the goggle eyes.
➤ Show the children how to glue one end of ribbon behind each foot and the other half way up the back of the robin.
➤ Stick three sticky pads on the back of the robin and press firmly on to the backing card.

Support and extension

Help younger children to draw around the templates and cut out the cardboard shapes. Invite older children to share templates and take turns to do the different parts. Let them decorate the background card with white glitter.

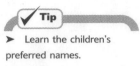

Tip

➤ Learn the children's preferred names.

Evaluation

It is okay for each robin to be individual. Some may be larger, smaller or an irregular shape and may bear little relationship to the picture. The process is more important than the end product and the children should be allowed to develop the project to their satisfaction.

Supporting activity

Talk to the children about what makes them feel happy in the home and in the setting.

➤ **Case study**

Nikhil is a nervous child who has taken a long time to settle down in the setting. Unfortunately workmen are due to come into the setting the following week to replace the central heating system and you are worried how Nikhil will respond. The nursery will have to move into another part of the building temporarily. How can you prepare and reassure Nikhil for these changes? Write down the case study with your responses for your portfolio.

E1.3: 1, 2, 3 ◄

➤ **Follow on**

Make a list of the causes of anxieties children may experience. Not all children will experience the same difficulties; age will play a part, as will the children's personalities. Include things like thunder, the dark and dogs. Give some indication of how you can lessen the distress. Put in your portfolio.

E1.3: 3 ◄

Questions

(See answer pointers at end of chapter.)

➤ 7. *What sort of comfort objects may children bring into the setting with them* · · · · *E1.3*: 4 ◄
as a form of reassurance, and where may they be kept?

➤ 8. *How can children develop a sense of belonging to the setting?* · · · · · · · · *E1.3*: 5 ◄

➤ 9. *In what ways can cultural diversity be shown in the setting to reflect the* · · · · · *E1.3*: 6 ◄
backgrounds of the children?

Record the questions and your full answers and share these with your assessor.

Did you know?

There are many reasons why young children become anxious, according to Dr Richard Woolfson in his book *A–Z of Child Development* (Stoddart Publishers, 1995). Dr Woolfson says that failing to get something right in nursery, having a poor relationship with parents, being reprimanded by mum and dad, not being invited to a birthday party, catching a cold, noticing that a pet is unwell or a family bereavement, can all undermine a young child's sense of well-being.

Extra idea

➤ Use puppets as a means to communicate with a child distressed by change. · · · · *E1.3*: 3 ◄

Practical ways of collecting evidence

Make a photographic record of the physical environment, both indoors and out. This can show the layout of furniture, equipment and safety features. Glue photographs on a page in such a way that you can make comments around the edge to indicate what is there. Show displays you have been involved with and noticeboards you may be responsible for. Put in your portfolio.

Check your progress

For this Unit you are expected to be directly observed by your assessor, under real working conditions, for at least one aspect of each Range statement for each of the three Elements. Other aspects may be observed, but if this is not possible you will need to collect evidence for Performance Criteria by other means. This may be through an inspection of the setting to assess your role in maintaining the physical environment, photographic records, reflective accounts of your experiences, witness testimonies indicating work you have done when the assessor is not there, plans and child observations.

Answer pointers

Ensure your answers are fully made for your assessor.

1. Stable. Right size. Space to move around. Suitable for activities. Accessible. Rounded edges. Safe. Strong.

2. Setting the table. Selecting toys. Tidying up. Handing round drinks. Caring for animals. Watering plants. Hanging coats on pegs.

3. More variety. Stimulate activities. Respond to children. Changing needs. Accommodating children with special needs.

4. Stimulation. Discussion. Extending language. Knowledge and understanding. Catching interests.

5. Non-toxic. Supervision. Health and safety policy. Safely displayed.

6. Bring from home. Home-setting link. In discussion. Set task. Children's suggestions. Children's interest.

7. Dummy. Rag. Blanket. Ribbon. Teddy. Feeding bottle. Personal drawer or basket. High shelf. Cupboard. Safe. Individual bag.

8. Personalised objects. Cup. Toothbrush. Peg with name on. Drawer with name on. Name on displayed items. Greeted by name.

9. Home corner. Positive images. Posters. Photographs. Language used. Familiar artefacts.

Further information

Festival Displays, Language Displays, Our World Displays, All About Me Displays, Maths Displays, Seasonal Displays, Story and Rhyme Displays and Science Displays all in *Themes on Display* series
(Scholastic, 2000)

A–Z of Child Development: From Birth to Five Years
Dr Richard Woolfson
(Stoddart Publishers, 1995)

E2 Maintain the safety and security of children

This Unit refers to ensuring a safe environment for children, including when on outings. There are Elements on accident prevention, child protection and emergency procedures. Supervision is also covered.

This chapter will enable you to:

E2.1 Maintain a safe environment for children
E2.2 Maintain the supervision of children
E2.3 Carry out emergency procedures
E2.4 Cope with accidents and injuries to children
E2.5 Help protect children from abuse
E2.6 Maintain the safety of children on outings.

Element E2.1 Maintain a safe environment for children

➤ Your assessor can observe and question you. · **E2.1**: Range 1a, b ◄

Safe and sound

Evidence for this Element will be covered by direct observations, over a number of visits, by your assessor and can be cross-referenced. The observations will be carried out as part of the regular routine and should demonstrate good practice.

What to do

➤ Clean surfaces thoroughly when preparing for a food activity.
➤ Ensure surfaces are cleaned following messy activities, such as painting, printing or gluing.
➤ Wash baby toys regularly to prevent cross infection.
➤ Always use equipment correctly, for its intended purpose.
➤ Select materials for activities that are appropriate to the children's developmental level.
➤ Use materials designed for the purpose, such as washable children's glue and non-toxic paint.
➤ Every time you take out a toy or piece of equipment, check that it is safe and undamaged.
➤ Remove any damaged items and refer to your supervisor. Record in the appropriate place, according to the procedure of the setting.
➤ Place waste materials in appropriate containers ready for collection.
➤ Ensure all gates, doors and windows are safely fastened.
➤ Use socket covers and fireguards. Ensure there are no trailing flexes.
➤ Make sure access is clear to rooms and fire doors.

✔ **Tip**

➤ Give all equipment a 'spring clean' on a rotational basis. Any large-scale cleaning requirements outside your remit should be referred to your supervisor.

E2.1: 1, 2

➤ Ensure that dressing-up clothes are washed regularly.

E2.1.1

Support and extension

Basic health and safety procedures should be appropriate to the children's developmental level. Extra precautions may need to be taken if you have children with special needs.

Evaluation

As an assistant in the setting you will have a defined role. Do you know exactly what is expected of you regarding the safety of the environment in your setting? Are there other tasks you can do? Do you know the correct procedures for these tasks?

Supporting activity

Familiarise yourself with the relevant health and safety policies for your setting. Discuss procedures and good practice with your colleagues and carry out competently.

➤ **E2.1**: 1, 2, 4, 5, 6, · · · ·
7, 8, 9, 10

Case study

After building work, the room has been left dusty and disorganised. A cleaning team has been in to spring clean the room, the flooring and the furniture. With a colleague you have now been asked to put everything in its place, ensure all the toys and equipment are clean and all the safety equipment is satisfactory and in place. Detail how you will set about doing this, what safety equipment is required and what issues need addressing, to report to your supervisor. Write down the case study with your responses for your portfolio.

➤ **E2.1**: 3 · · · · · · · ·

Follow on

Consider the safety equipment requirements for different age groups in diverse settings. Prepare a table with four columns, headed 'equipment', 'nursery', 'school' and 'home'. Write the list in the first column and place a tick in the other three if you feel that a piece of equipment is likely to be needed in that type of setting.

early years
*training &
management*

Questions

(See answer pointers at end of chapter.)

➤ **1.** *What materials do you need to clean and maintain equipment and surfaces?* · · · **E2.1**: 1 ◄

➤ **2.** *What waste materials are produced in childcare settings and how should they* · · **E2.1**: 7 ◄
be disposed of?

➤ **3.** *What are the potential hazards you need to be aware of in your setting?* · · · · · **E2.1**: 8 ◄

Record the questions and your full answers and share these with your assessor.

Did you know?

Life was much more difficult in Victorian times. This quotation from *Enquire Within Upon Everything* (Houlston and Sons, 1894) illustrates that the following 'may always be applied so as to restore the pristine beauty of the furniture by a little manual labour. Heat a gallon of water, in which dissolve one pound and a half of potash; and a pound of virgin wax, boiling the whole for half an hour, then suffer it to cool, when the wax will float on the surface. Put the wax into a mortar, and triturate it with a marble pestle, adding soft water to it until it forms a soft paste, which, laid neatly on furniture, or even on paintings, and carefully rubbed when dry with a woollen rag, gives a polish of great brilliancy...'. No more complaints then?

Extra idea

➤ If you have found a fault in equipment, furniture or play materials and it has been — **E2.1**: 5 ◄
reported and recorded, photocopy the relevant page and put in your portfolio.

Element E2.2 Maintain the supervision of children

➤ Your assessor can observe and question you. · · · · · · · · · · · · · · · · · · · **E2.2**: *Range 1a, b* ◄

Water activities

Water is a potential hazard for all young children. It is also great fun and positive learning experiences can come from it. The significant factor attached to water play, other than with very small amounts, is supervision. *Number of children: from individual children to small groups.*

Resources

Water; towels; containers and other resources as identified.

Preparation

Plan the activity using the 'Activity preparation' photocopiable sheet on page 121. Ask your setting supervisor for support in doing this if necessary. Ensure the resources required are available prior to the start of the activity. Have towels ready to prevent chilling. The children may need waterproof aprons for some of the activities.

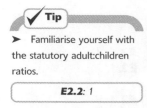

➤ Familiarise yourself with the statutory adult:children ratios.

E2.2: 1

➤ Explain the rules of safety, rather than stopping children from doing potentially dangerous things.

E2.2: 5

What to do

➤ Provide a bowl of water for children to experience floating and sinking objects, such as sponges, corks, stones, shells, plastic ducks and nuts.
➤ Bath dolls in a baby bath filled with water.
➤ Squirt patterns on the playground or patio using water in clean, empty washing-up liquid containers.
➤ Dig channels in the sand to pour water along.
➤ Invite the children to 'paint' an outside wall using buckets of plain water and a house painting brush.
➤ Colour water with food colourings, putting different colours in different containers. Add together in the water tray to experiment with colour mixing.
➤ Spring clean the dolls' clothes in a sink of soapy water.

Support and extension

Choose activities suitable for the developmental level of the children, the physical environment and the number of adults available for supervision.

Evaluation

Could the children experiment with the water with a minimum of supervision? Did you adequately supervise the activity? How can you offer the activity in a different way in the future? Did the children get wet when you intended them to keep dry? How can you avoid this in the future? Did you get wet? How did you feel about this?

Supporting activity

Develop a freezing and melting session with the children. Freeze water in an ice-cube tray and use the cubes in drinks. Freeze a large block of water in an ice-cream tub and put it outside to melt. Check it regularly and record how long it takes to melt.

➤ **E2.2**: 1, 2, 3, 4, 5, · · · ·
6, 7, cross-reference
to **P1**

Case study

Megan loves climbing. She expresses no fear and will climb on to walls, to the top of the climbing frame, scramble the climbing net and even up the bookshelves. On one occasion she was found on the shed roof. Her mother is quite indulgent and makes no attempt to stop her. How will you approach this situation and what strategies will you use? Write down the case study with your responses for your portfolio.

➤ **E2.2**: 1, 3, 7 · · · · · · ·

Follow on

Consider the various activities that require extra vigilance. Ask yourself whether there are small items the children can swallow, push up their nose or poke in their ear? Think of larger equipment a child can fall off or those toys that can be used to hit someone with. Water can prove hazardous and sand can get in their eyes and hair. Screens can be pushed over, carpets can be tripped over and children can be pushed into furniture. Adequate supervision, without over-protecting, is important wherever young children are. Look around your setting and assess where potential hazards are and where adults are needed to supervise. Share your findings with your assessor.

Questions

(See answer pointers at end of chapter.)

➤ **E2.2**: 1, 2, 4, 5, 6, 7, 8   **4.** *Identify the rules of supervision that a practitioner should follow.*

➤ **5.** *How can you raise the children's awareness about safety?* · · · · · · · · · · **E2.2**: 6 ◄
➤ **6.** *In what ways does over-protection of children damage them?* · · · · · · · · · · **E2.2**: 7 ◄

Record the questions and your full answers and share these with your assessor.

Did you know?
Children have drowned in as little as 5 cm of water.

Extra idea
➤ At home time supervise the children until their parents or carers collect them. · · · **E2.2**: 8, *cross-reference* ◄
Ask a colleague to sign a witness testimony to confirm your involvement. *to* **P1**

Element E2.3 Carry out emergency procedures

➤ Your assessor can observe and question you. · · · · · · · · · · · · · · · · · **E2.3**: *Range 1a, b,* ◄
2a, b

Emergency checklist
Number of children: whole group.

What to do
➤ Familiarise yourself with the policies and procedures of your setting.
➤ Confirm your role, so you know exactly what you are expected to do.
➤ Find out if there are different alerts for different emergencies, such as an electronic bell for a fire alarm and a hand bell for a bomb alert.
➤ Identify all the emergency exits and how to open them.
➤ Ensure there is unobstructed access to all entrances and exits.
➤ Check where the fire extinguishers are and how to use them.
➤ Locate other emergency equipment, such as fire blankets and fire hoses.
Find out when and how each of these should be used.
➤ Establish where the smoke alarms are in your setting.
➤ Find out where contact details for parents are kept.
➤ Be certain you know where the assembly point is for you and the children.
➤ Practise until you feel sure you could undertake your duties in an emergency in a safe and satisfactory manner.
➤ Ask who you should report any difficulties with emergency procedures to.
➤ Find out if visitors to your setting have to sign in and out.

Tip

➤ Watch a relevant video or read a book with the children, such as Fireman Sam, and discuss the dangers featured. Be aware of the fear that children may have.

Support and extension

Each setting will do things differently. Find out the exact expectations from your setting.

Evaluation

Do you feel confident that you know what to do in an emergency evacuation? Do you know where to go if you are with the children in a different area of the building? In a real emergency your colleagues will have their own responsibilities; you must know yours before the event.

Supporting activity

If there are children with special educational needs in your setting find out what you need to do if they are with you when an emergency is called.

➤ **E2.3**: 1, 5, 6 . . . . . .

Case study

The fire bell sounds while you are with three children in the cloakroom. Connor starts to panic, cries and hides in the corner. How will you deal with the situation? What are your priorities? Describe the sequence of events in chronological order. Write down the case study with your responses for your portfolio. ◄

➤ **E2.3**: 1, 2, 3, 4, 6 · · ·

Follow on

Make a list of all the emergencies that can happen in a setting, including emergencies due to fire, water, electricity and weather. Ask yourself 'what if' questions and think through how you should respond. What if the river burst its banks and floods your setting? What if the power fails on a dark winter day? Think of more and write them down with your responses. Put in your portfolio. ◄

Questions

(See answer pointers at end of chapter.)

➤ **E2.3**: 2 . . . .
7. *How will you find out about emergency procedures and the use of equipment? What responsibility will you take after gaining this information?* ◄

➤ **E2.3**: 5, 7 · · · · · · ·
8. *What situations do you expect to report and what response do you anticipate?* ◄

➤ **E2.3**: 6 · · · · · · · ·
9. *How are you personally expected to respond to an emergency evacuation?* ◄

Record the questions and your full answers and share these with your assessor.

Did you know?

Every year 75 children die and more than 2000 are injured in house fires.

Extra idea

➤ **E2.3**: 7 · · · · · · · ·
If your name is recorded on any documentation, such as emergency record books or forms, make a copy and put in your portfolio. ◄

Element E2.4 Cope with accidents and injuries to children

➤ Your assessor can observe and question you. · **E2.4**: *Range 2a, b* ◄

999

Children can be prepared for accidents by raising their awareness of the causes and how best to treat them if they occur.
Number of children: four.

Resources

Four enlarged card copies of the '999' photocopiable sheet on page 132; scissors; small bandages; plasters; cotton wool balls; plastic gloves; triangular bandage; eye patches; matchboxes; white paper; glue or sticky tape; green felt-tipped pen; dice; dolls (optional).

Preparation

Cut out the 999 counters and fold along the lines so they stand up. Cover the matchboxes with white paper and glue down. Draw a green cross on each side to make a miniature first aid box.

What to do

➤ Give each child a copy of the game sheet, a 999 counter and eight small first-aid objects. These could be stored in the miniature first aid boxes you have made.
➤ Place the objects in any order on the squares numbered 1 to 8.
➤ Invite the children to take turns to throw the dice and move their counters around the board according to the numbers shown.
➤ Depending on the developmental level of the children, invite them to respond in different ways.
  ♦ Ask the child to name the object and describe its use, with help if necessary.
  ♦ Ask the child to name the object and mime its use.
  ♦ Ask the child to name the object and demonstrate its use, either on a doll or another child. Let the children help one another apply 'first aid'.
➤ Once a square has been landed on, remove the object.
➤ The winner is the first one to reach the 999 square.

✓ Tip
➤ Treat all accidents as potentially serious until they have been checked.

E2.4: 3

Support and extension

Discuss accidents and first aid with the children. Remind them how uncomfortable it is when they hurt themselves. Talk about how they can avoid accidents.

Evaluation
Was the game pitched at the right level for the children? Was it fun? Did a serious message come across? How else can you play the game? Did the activity suggest spontaneous play opportunities for the children? Were opportunities for language development explored?

Supporting activity
Provide nurses outfits, white coats and paramedic outfits for the children to dress up in. Outfits can be made from old plain shirts.

➤ **E2.4**: 3, 4, 6, 7 · · · ·

Case study
Keziah has fallen outside and is sitting tearfully on the ground nursing a grazed knee. A small group of children have gathered around to see what has happened. How will you respond? Where and how will you deal with it? Write down the case study with your responses for your portfolio.

➤ **E2.4**: 1, 2 · · · · · ·

Follow on
Check the first aid box in your setting. Make a note of the contents, how often it is checked, who checks it and how it is replenished. Make a note of your findings and share with your assessor.

Questions
(See answer pointers at end of chapter.)

➤ **E2.4**: 5 · · · · · · · · **10.** *How can you prevent the spread of infection when dealing with accidents and emergencies?*

➤ **E2.4**: 6, 8 · · · · · · · **11.** *How can you reassure a distressed, injured child? Who needs to be informed?*

➤ **E2.4**: 7 · · · · · · · · **12.** *What conditions are defined as accidents or medical emergencies and why?*

Record the questions and your full answers and share these with your assessor.

Did you know?
According to the Children Act Regulations the setting must keep a signed record of all accidents to children and notify OFSTED of any serious injury or death of a child or adult on the premises.

Extra idea
➤ **E2.4**: 3 · · · · · · · · Enrol on a first aid course. Include any certificates and details of the course in your portfolio.

Element E2.5 Help protect children from abuse

It is not expected that you will be directly observed for this Element. This activity may create an opportunity for spontaneous comments from the children about their bodies, to raise issues about child abuse. It can be cross-referenced to C8.

➤ **E2.5**: 5 · · · · · · · · Your assessor can question you.

Jiggling skeleton
Number of children: six.

Resources
Thin card copy of 'Skeleton' photocopiable sheet on page 133; brass open-out paper clips; black felt-tipped pens, single hole punch or pointed scissors; children's scissors; sticky tape; strong straws.

Preparation
Plan the activity using the 'Activity preparation' photocopiable sheet on page 121. Ask your setting supervisor for support in doing this if necessary.

What to do
➤ Invite the children to colour in the skeleton pieces, leaving all the bone areas white.
➤ Help the children cut out the sections of the skeleton around the outlines.
➤ Using the hole punch or pointed scissors, help the children to make holes where indicated by the black dots.
➤ Encourage the children to assemble the skeleton by pushing the brass clips through the relevant two pieces so the parts swing freely.
➤ Let the children sticky-tape a straw to the back to jiggle the skeleton.

Support and extension
Help the children make the holes for the paper clips. Enlarge the copy of the skeleton to help younger children manage the intricate details. Challenge older children to make up a jiggling skeleton puppet play. Care should be taken with the sharp ends of the paper clips.

Evaluation
Were the children able to follow your instructions? Did they suggest ways of using the skeleton for other purposes? Were you able to raise issues about their bodies? Did you receive the support of a colleague for this activity?

Supporting activity
Let the children make up the 'Skeleton' photocopiable sheet on page 133 and dress the body in a swimsuit, by colouring in or using tissue paper clothes. Talk about the body, its component parts and how it works, reinforcing the message that the children's bodies belong to themselves. Work with a colleague if you do not feel confident with this activity.

Tip
➤ Confidentiality is the key word. Aspects of your work must not be discussed with anyone outside the work setting and then only to the appropriate people.

E2.5: 6

Case study
➤ Tomás is usually a chatty, friendly, responsive child. However since a new 'uncle' has come to live with him and his mother his behaviour has changed. He seems withdrawn and nervous. When you help him to change for PE you notice three small round wounds on his back. They look like burns, but you cannot imagine how they got there. What may be the cause of the change in behaviour and the injuries on his back? What do you think should happen next? Write down the case study with your responses for your portfolio.

E2.5: 1, 2, 3, 4, 5, 6 ◄

Follow on
➤ Children can be hurt in different ways. Consider a range of them. Children may fall in the playground, bang their heads on tables or receive sports injuries. They may be bullied, emotionally hurt or physically and sexually abused. Find out what the signs and symptoms are. Do not judge or jump to conclusions and refer to more experienced people to investigate.

E2.5: 1, 4, 5 ◄

Questions

(See answer pointers at end of chapter.)

➤ **E2.5**: 1 . . . . **13.** *What opportunities are available, in the regular routine, for you to notice bruises, injuries and abrasions?* ◀

➤ **E2.5**: 5 . . . . **14.** *What circumstances may give cause for concern and how can you deal with the situation?* ◀

➤ **E2.5**: 6 . . . . **15.** *Why is confidentiality so important within the setting, especially with regard to child protection?* ◀

Record the questions and your full answers and share these with your assessor.

Did you know?

In England and Wales around 80 children are killed in the home every year.

Extra idea

➤ **E2.5**: 5 . . . . Read stories to the children about bullying. If any comments are raised that may indicate a cause for concern, refer to your supervisor. Keep a record of such incidents with the date and concern, but without identifying the child. Attach it to a witness testimony and put in your portfolio. ◀

Element E2.6 Maintain the safety of children on outings

Your assessor may not be present when you accompany the children on an outing. You may need to get a witness testimony for this Element. You can extend the children's awareness and memory by bringing leaves back with you (see below). However, this later activity will not provide evidence for E2.6, as it is a follow-on activity. If observed it will provide evidence for C8.

➤ **E2.6**: Range 1a, 2a, · · Your assessor can question you. ◀
b, c, 3a, b, c,
4a, b

Leaf printing

Number of children: six.

Resources

Collection of flat whole leaves, preferably collected on a walk; paint; brushes; large sheet of paper; plate; kitchen; block of firm sponge, or thick card; double-sided sticky tape; paper.

Preparation

Plan the activity by completing the 'Activity preparation' photocopiable sheet on page 121. You may need to do this with the support of your supervisor in the setting. Fold a pad of kitchen paper, place it on a plate, and pour over a thin layer of paint to create a paint pad.

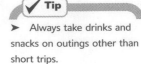

✓ **Tip**

➤ Always take drinks and snacks on outings other than short trips.

E2.6: 7

What to do

➤ Ensure everything you use is safe; keep leaves away from the mouth and eyes.
➤ Help the children to make printing blocks with the firm sponge. Stick double sided tape to one side of the leaf (it could be the back or the front as they produce different results – try both ways), and stick to the block.
➤ Press on the paint pad on the plate.
➤ Print the design on the paper.
➤ Encourage the children to be creative in their designs.
➤ Produce a relief pattern leaf by placing the leaf on the paper, holding down firmly with finger tips, and paint over the edges with a brush. Carefully remove the leaf to show the outline.

Support and extension

You will need to help the younger children to make their printing blocks. Older children can use their imagination. When the paint is dry they can draw faces on the leaves, on the leaf relief, or make them into animals.

Evaluation

Did you discuss where the leaves were from? Did you prompt children to remind them of incidents on the walk? Were the children able to demonstrate their creativity with the leaf prints? Did they have the competencies for making their own printing blocks. Did they make other suggestions for printing?

Supporting activities

If you have a garden, collect a selection of safe leaves from different plants to share with the children. Invite young children to stick them to card. Go for a walk in the garden and see if they can match the leaves up to the right plants. Press Plasticine along the bottom of a plastic box and a little way up the sides. Press one or more leaves down hard, without overlapping, to create an imprint and then remove. Mix some plaster of Paris and pour a thick layer over the Plasticine. Leave to dry for 24 hours, then carefully remove the Plasticine. You will be left with a permanent record of your collection that can be painted. Place a leaf upside down and cover with a sheet of paper. Holding firmly to prevent it moving, rub the side of a wax crayon over the sheet until the leaf shape and veins appear.

➤ **Case study**

As you have been gaining confidence in the setting, your supervisor wishes to give you more experience. With a colleague, you have been asked to organise an outing to a local farm park. There will be 16 children, five members of staff and some parents. You have been delegated to prepare the letter informing the parents of the proposed trip. The letter must include space to collect the relevant information required from the parents. What factors do you need to consider, what do you need to arrange and what do you have to do to prepare for this trip? Write down the case study with your responses for your portfolio.

E2.6: 1, 2, 3, 4, 5, 8, 9, ◄ cross-reference to **P1**

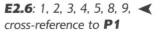

➤ *Cross-reference to* · · · ·
P1 *and* **P9**

Follow on
Practise drawing up draft letters informing parents of different events.
Put them in your portfolio.

Questions
(See answer pointers at end of chapter.)

➤ **E2.6**: *2, 3* · · · · · · · **16.** *What permission is needed before taking the children out and what contact information is required while on the outing?*

➤ **E2.6**: *6* · · · · · · · · **17.** *What equipment and clothing is appropriate to take with you on an outing?*

➤ **E2.6**: *8* · · · · · · · · **18.** *Before taking the children on an outing, what considerations do you need to make with regard to walking, public transport and private transport?*

Record the questions and your full answers and share these with your assessor.

Did you know?
Oak trees support as many as 284 insect species. Encourage children to think small when investigating nature.

Extra idea

➤ **E2.6**: *10* · · · · · · · Using the 'Spider chart' photocopiable sheet on page 122, write 'Outing incidents' in the centre. In each surrounding box write an incident with a brief description of your role in resolving the situation.

Practical ways of collecting evidence
Part of your role is to ensure you are carrying out health and safety procedures to the satisfaction of the assessor. Most of the Performance Criteria in **E2.1** and **E2.2** will be observed when you are undertaking your regular routine and will not need to be set up specifically. Ensure your assessor has noted this on the direct observation sheet so it can be cross-referenced into the appropriate Unit.

Check your progress
You are expected to be directly observed for at least one aspect of each of the Range statements in **E2.1**, **E2.2** and **E2.3**. Direct observation for the other three Elements may not be possible, although you can, of course, collect direct observations if the occasion arises. Evidence must therefore be collected in alternative ways, such as an inspection of the setting, work products, policies and procedures for your assessor to question you on. Write reflective accounts when events happen, get signed witness testimonies and put in your portfolio case studies and assignments. If you are unable to collect certain evidence, such as emergency procedures and accidents, simulations may be set up in the setting or by a training agency.

Answer pointers

Ensure your answers are fully made for your assessor.

1. Hot soapy water. Bowl. Disposable cloths. Paper towels. Antibacterial spray. Sterilising fluid. Small scrubbing brush.

2. Nappies. Paper towels. Kitchen waste. General rubbish. Paper. Bottles. Female personal hygiene waste. Tissues. Wipes. Cotton wool. Nappy bags. Wheelie bins. Clinical waste. Recycling centres.

3. Water. Chemicals. Glass. Animals. Strangers. Gardening equipment. Slippery floors. Uneven surfaces. Traffic. Hot ovens. Heaters. Doors.

4. Sufficient staff. Calm. Relaxed. Promote self-confidence. Do not undermine. Explanation. Increase awareness. Not over-protected. Known adults. Policies.

5. Explain rules. Remind. Restrict access. Prohibit.

6. Reduces self-esteem. Limits children. Reduces experience. Limits skills. Limits exploration. Can stereotype.

7. Evacuation procedures on wall. Emergency equipment. Use instructions by equipment. Policies and procedures. Read. Ask questions. Search out.

8. Incidents. Difficulties. Missing notices. Accurate. Recorded. Appropriate action.

9. Calmly. Competently. Promptly. Accurately. According to instruction.

10. Wash hands. Sterile dressings. Cover wound. Disposable gloves. Disinfectant. Antibacterial spray. Waste disposal.

11. Talk. Reassure. Comfort. Cuddle. Distract. Explain. Colleague. Supervisor. Parent. Medical personnel. Paramedics.

12. Severe bleeding. Burns. Choking. Poisoning. Scalding. Unconsciousness. Bad fall. Life threatening. Severe injury. Urgent. Needs medication.

13. Toileting. Observation. Potty training. Changing for PE. Nappy changing. Observation of exposed areas, such as hands and face.

14. Unexplained injury. Parent and child giving different reasons. Disclosure. Round cigarette burns. Injuries in unusual places, such as inner thigh and inner upper arm. Strap or cane marks. Report. Record.

15. Protect child. Personal. Non-judgemental. No gossiping. No jumping to conclusions. Investigation. Respect.

16. Parental. Head of setting. Parents' names. Telephone numbers. Emergency contact numbers. Details of children, such as date of birth, address, GP. Setting telephone number.

17. Coats, hats, wellington boots. Umbrellas. Buggies. Prams. Reins. Rope.

18. Know the route. Times. Availability. Insurance. Numbers. Adults available. Distance. Car seats. Booster seats. Seat belts.

Further information

Listening to Young Children
Alison Clark and Peter Moss
(Joseph Rowntree Foundation and the National Children's Bureau, 2001)

Ourselves
Anne Pratt, Neil Griffiths and Sylvia Wright (Nelson Thornes, 2001)

Natural Childhood: A Practical Guide to The First Seven Years
John B Thomson (Gaia Books Limited, 1995)

Safety for Home-Based Child Care: Guidelines for Childminders
Rosie Mercer (Child Accident Prevention Trust, 2001)

M3 Contribute to the achievement of organisational requirements

This Unit covers aspects of working with others as part of an organisation. It refers to the role and responsibilities of the candidate and familiarisation with the organisation's structure. It also covers professional development, self-knowledge and how to deal with conflict in the organisation. You are expected to carry out your duties in a satisfactory manner, give feedback and relate to colleagues in the work setting. Tasks to be covered include setting out and clearing away activities, preparing materials for activities, maintaining the environment and supervising activities.

This chapter will enable you to:
M3.1 Carry out instructions and provide feedback
M3.2 Contribute to the development of good practice.

Element M3.1 Carry out instructions and provide feedback

➤ *M3.1: Range 1a,* · · · · *2a, b, c, d*

The supervisor is the person you report to and who gives you instructions. Your assessor can observe and question you.

Making mini gardens
Imagine your supervisor has asked you to:
➤ Design and make mini gardens
➤ Collect materials and prepare the area
➤ Ask four children to make gardens
➤ Lead the children through what they are to do
➤ Supervise the activity, allowing the children to make their own choices and their own design
➤ Promote language development by discussion
➤ Display the finished gardens
➤ Clear the resources away and clean the area
➤ Complete the activity within an agreed timescale.

Number of children: four.

Resources
Four plastic vegetable trays; compost; bowl; small mirrors or kitchen foil; stones; fine gravel; grass seed; short twigs; Plasticine; small world people; small jug; water; card; pen.

early years training & management

Preparation

Plan the activity using the 'Activity preparation' photocopiable sheet on page 121. Ask your setting supervisor for support in doing this if necessary. Identify a suitable area and gather the materials together. Put some compost in the bowl and water in the jug.

Tip

➤ Time management is important. Practise being efficient and keeping within expected timescales.

M3.1: 4

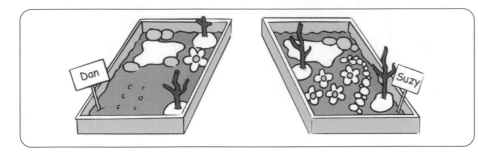

What to do

➤ Explain that the group will be making mini gardens.
➤ Ask the children to put a layer of compost in their plastic trays.
➤ Let the children develop their gardens. If necessary, suggest uses for the materials, such as mirrors or foil for a pond, twigs in a Plasticine base for trees, stones for a path or pond edging, Plasticine flowers and grass seed to grow. They do not have to use all the materials.
➤ Label the trays with the children's names and water the seeds if used.
➤ Let the children display their gardens on a shelf or table and share with parents at home time.

Support and extension

Let younger children create their garden freely. There may be no paths or apparent design, however it is *their* design. Older children can use additional resources, such as lolly sticks to make an archway or building bricks as seats.

Evaluation

Were you able to follow your supervisor's instructions? Did you find all the resources you needed? Did you clarify instructions if you were unsure? Did you let the children develop their own design? Did you offer encouragement? Did you promote language development through discussion and by introducing new words? Did you finish within the agreed timescale?

Supporting activity

Keep your own record of instructions, such as your routine responsibilities and your role in an emergency. Show your assessor.

> ➤ **Case study**
> Your supervisor wants to assess how well you are working. She asks you to prepare the role-play area as a hairdressing salon, labelling and setting out brushes, mirrors, combs and accessories, as well as making relevant signs. She would also like you to supervise the children playing in the hairdressers. After the session you need to report on what you did and how the children used the activity. Detail how you would set up the activity, what you might see the children doing and what you will report back to the supervisor. Write down the case study with your responses for your portfolio.

M3.1: 1, 2, 5, 6, 7 ◀

➤ **M3.1**: 4, 6, 7, 9, 10 · ·

Follow on
Ask for feedback on your involvement in activities. Ask your supervisor to make a record of the feedback. Suggest how to improve your input next time. Make sure your supervisor and you sign the record and place in your portfolio. Once you feel confident on how feedback is given, practise giving feedback to others, using the same method for recording. Put this in your portfolio.

Questions
(See answer pointers at end of chapter.)

➤ **M3.1**: 1, 2, 7, 8 · · · · **1.** *What principles should you follow when you are given written or verbal instruction?*

➤ **M3.1**: 2, 8, 9 · · · · · **2.** *If you are unsure about instructions, experience difficulties following instructions or need additional support, who should you discuss this with?*

➤ **M3.1**: 10 · · · · · · · **3.** *What are the boundaries of confidentiality within the setting, and why?*

Record questions and your full answers and share with your assessor.

Did you know?
The dictionary defines 'instruction' as 'information, direction and command'. It defines 'feedback' as 'response or reaction providing useful information or guidelines for further development'. So putting the two together becomes a cycle of quality, where you are given instruction, act on it, give feedback to others, who in turn give feedback to you relating to those actions. The aim is an ongoing improvement of your practice in the setting.

Extra idea

➤ **M3.1**: 1, 2 · · · · · · · Do an information audit of the setting. Note how many notices there are, such as the fire drill, photocopier instructions and book borrowing information, and where they are. Note visitor instructions, policy documents and health and safety information. If you do not understand any aspect of the information, ask your supervisor and record the responses.

Element M3.2 Contribute to the development of good practice

➤ **M3.2**: Range 1a, b · · · Your assessor can observe and question you.

Assisting in PE sessions
Number of children: small group or whole group.

Resources
PE equipment as identified by your supervisor.

Preparation
Follow the instructions given by your supervisor.

What to do
➤ Read and ensure you understand the setting's policies for this activity.
➤ Set up the equipment in the places identified.

➤ Move heavy equipment in a safe manner, following good practice on manual handling. If are not sure ask your supervisor.

➤ Check each piece of equipment as you put it out. Remove any damaged items and report to your supervisor.

➤ Supervise the children as they participate in the activity.

➤ Join in to encourage the children. Check they use the equipment safely and follow your instructions.

➤ Clear the equipment safely away at the end of the session. Let the children help with smaller equipment.

➤ Report any difficulties or suggestions for improvement to your supervisor.

Tip
➤ Ask if you can shadow an experienced member of staff to see how things are expected to be done.

Support and extension

Consider the layout of the equipment, giving reasons for any changes. Look into different age groups, abilities and equipment available. If music has been used, can you suggest an alternative piece?

Evaluation

How can you contribute to good practice in this activity? Can you benefit from further training in this area, particularly manual handling? What should you do if a colleague puts their, and your, health at risk by not following correct procedures?

Supporting activity

➤ Seek permission from your supervisor to organise a PE session outdoors. Chalk a route of large shapes on the playground. Explain that the children have to reach each shape by different actions. For example, hop to a square, run to a circle and skip to a triangle.

Cross-reference to **C1** ◄

Case study

➤ As part of your training you go to an early years exhibition. You see many good products and some interesting ideas, including a demonstration using recycled and cheap materials to make displays. You have not seen this approach in the setting and feel it will be beneficial. The setting does not have much spare money and, as you have responsibility for displays, you will suggest using these materials. Who will you speak to and how will you make the recommendation without treading on anyone's toes? Write down the case study with your responses for your portfolio.

M3.2: 1, 2, 3, 4, 5, 7 ◄

Follow on

➤ You may not feel it is the right time to suggest changes to your supervisor, however you can discuss your ideas with your assessor. Every new teacher, leader or supervisor likes to try new ways of working. If you were in charge of the setting, what changes might you make? Explain your reasons.

M3.2: 1, 2, 3, 4, 5, 7 ◄

Questions

(See answer pointers at end of chapter.)

➤ **4.** *If you are offered training to work with children with special education needs, or in an area you are unfamiliar with, how will you respond and why?*

M3.2: 5 ◄

➤ **5.** *What will you do if you notice a colleague is not following the setting policy?*

M3.2: 6 ◄

➤ **6.** *What information sources can you share with colleagues that contribute to good practice?*

M3.2: 7 ◄

Record questions and your full answers and share with your assessor.

Did you know?

An old proverb says 'practice makes perfect'. So by repeating a skill over and over again you get better at it. For the childcare and early years practitioner this means putting theory into practice and learning by your experience. In AD 108, the Roman administrator Pliny the Younger is reputed to have said 'it is difficult to retain the knowledge one has acquired, without putting it into practice'. This is still true today.

➤ **M3.2**: *1, 2, 3, 7* · · · ·

Extra idea

Attend staff meetings and contribute to the discussions. Draw on ideas from other settings, training courses, experience and your private study. You may wish to discuss your ideas with your supervisor beforehand. Highlight any contribution you have made and put in your portfolio.

Practical ways of collecting evidence

Much evidence for this Unit will be gained through activities and practice during the regular routine. Your assessor, who will want to see your competence on a day-to-day basis, will directly observe this. Your working relationship with others will be observed, as will your ability to follow instruction, report back, respond according to circumstances and contribute to good practice.

Check your progress

You are expected to be directly observed for at least one aspect of each of the range categories for **M3.1**, although you may cover more if you wish. It is not expected you will be directly observed for **M3.2**, although you must produce other forms of evidence. This can be gained through notes of instructions and other work products, reflective accounts of your work, preparation records for activities and programmes of activities. Witness testimonies can also be used.

Answer pointers

Ensure your answers are fully made for your assessor.

1. Listen. Read. Clarify. Within role. Report difficulties. Efficient. Consistent. Reliable.
2. Teacher. Supervisor. Line manager. Committee member.
3. Relevant work colleagues only. Respect. Libel. Supervisor. Privacy. Discretion.
4. Accept. Willing to learn. Positive. Adaptable. Flexible. Motivated.
5. Refer to relevant colleague. Be clear about policies. Follow correct procedure.
6. Products. Magazines. New regulations. Research. Organisations.

Further information

Early Years Care and Education NVQ/SNVQ Level 2 Workbook
(Hodder & Stoughton Educational, 1999)

P1   Relate to parents

This Unit focuses on interaction between practitioners and parents. It covers the basic requirements, reflecting the level of involvement with parents, to give effective care and education to the children. It promotes good practice in working with parents.

This chapter will enable you to:
P1.1 Interact and share information with parents about their children
P1.2 Share the care of children with their parents.

Element P1.1 Interact and share information with parents about their children

➤ Your assessor can observe and question you. · **P1.1**: *Range: 1a, b, 2a, b, c* ◄

Whose baby are you?
Number of children: small groups for discussion, whole group for display.

Resources
Photographs; display board; A4 paper; A5 skin tone paper; skin tone crayons; mirror; Blu-Tack; coloured backing paper; card labels.

Preparation
Ask your setting supervisor for support in planning this activity. Prepare a note to the parents requesting photographs of parents and their children, as babies. Ensure they have name labels. Ask the parents to list the sorts of toys they played with as a child. Cut large circles from A5 paper for each child.

What to do
➤ Talk to the children about growing up. Start with newborn babies and toddlers, how old they are now and eventually growing up to become adults.
➤ Talk to the children about the toys their parents used to play with. Discuss the similarities and differences to their toys today.
➤ Discuss how we change as we grow up.
➤ Look at the photographs together and ask the children to match up the parent with their child.
➤ Let the children look in a mirror to draw a self-portrait with the crayons.
➤ Attach the photographs and self-portraits to backing paper with Blu-Tack and display on the board.
➤ Invite the parents to view the display and tell them how well the children got on with the activity.

 **Tip**

➤ Be aware of the setting's policy and practices on interacting with parents. Clarify your role to avoid confusion.

P1.1: *1*

➤ Put up a multilingual poster welcoming parents to the setting.

P1.1: *1*

➤ If parents cannot communicate in English and you do not speak their language, find someone who can help you.

P1.1: *3*

➤ Parents are the experts on their own children.

 P1.1. *5*

Support and extension
Keep explanations simple for younger children. Look in the library for books showing the sort of toys the parents describe. Encourage older children to draw pictures of their toys today and their parents' toys.

➤ *Cross-reference to* **C4**

Evaluation
Did the parents praise the children? How else can you make parents feel comfortable in the setting? Were the parents actively involved in providing photographs and information? Did you feel confident in approaching the parents? Did the parents see the display and make comments? Were you able to discuss other issues with the parents?

Supporting activities
Make individual height charts for the children to take home. Ask the parents to bring old clothes in and peg to a washing line to compare different sizes. Start with baby clothes and move up to at least the size of the children in the setting. If possible, carry on up to adult sizes. This is a clear demonstration of growth.

➤ ***P1.1****: 1, 2, 3, 5, 6, · · · 7, 9*

Case study
Georgia's language is limited and you have difficulty understanding some of her words. She is obviously excited by something that has happened at home, but you are not clear what it is. It is something to do with 'bibi', although who or what 'bibi' is you are not sure. She is frustrated that you do not understand in this instance, although generally you find ways of communicating effectively. How will you approach her parents to find out what Georgia is trying to tell you, without dampening her enthusiasm or affecting her self-esteem? Write down the case study with your responses for your portfolio.

➤ *Cross-reference to* · · · **C9**

Follow on
Young children have their own ways of communicating with you. At first this is by crying, but soon other non-verbal methods are used, such as noises, pointing, taking you by the hand and leading you, nodding or shaking their head. Watch children to see what they do. Record five methods of non-verbal communication you have seen children use. Put in your portfolio.

Questions

(See answer pointers at end of chapter.)

➤ **1.** *What forms of address might parents prefer you to use when you talk to them?*   **P1.1**: 2   ◄

➤ **2.** *In what ways can you share information with parents to show them what their* · · **P1.1**: 6   ◄
child has been doing at the setting?

➤ **3.** *How can you draw parents' attention to their children's work to give them* · · · · **P1.1**: 8   ◄
encouragement and confidence?

Record the questions and your full answers and share these with your assessor.

Did you know?

The *Curriculum Guidance for the Foundation Stage* (DfEE, 2000) says 'Practitioners use a variety of ways to keep parents fully informed about the curriculum, such as brochures, displays and videos which are available in the home languages of the parents, and through informal discussion.'

Extra ideas

➤ Welcome the parents as they come into the setting. Be friendly, smile and use · · **P1.1**: 1, 2, 3, 4   ◄
their preferred name – refer to the 'Tips for naming names' photocopiable sheet on page 134. If parents ask you questions to which you can respond, give an accurate, competent and understandable reply. If you do not know the answer or it is not within your role, refer to the appropriate person.

➤ Make two lists, one with information about the setting for a parent and the other **P1.1**: 1, 3   ◄
requesting information from the parent for the setting. Gather any pre-printed information about the setting, such as policies, application forms and brochures, and explain why this information is prepared and needed.

➤ Find out about toy libraries in your area. Collect information and share with your **P1.1**: 3   ◄
parents. Put your findings in your portfolio.

Element P1.2 Share the care of children with their parents

➤ Your assessor can observe and question you. · · · · · · · · · · · · · · · · · · **P1.2**: *Range 1a, b*   ◄

Activity tasters for parents

It is valuable for parents to know what is happening in the setting when they are not there. Some parents lack practical childcare skills so inviting them in gives them the chance to learn and experience what the children can achieve. Many settings invite parents in for a play session to join in the activities with their children. Your role is to support and encourage the parents, talking them through the activities carried out in the setting.
Number of children: supervise small groups of children.

Resources

Resources according to the activities chosen, such as play dough (cross-reference to **C8.4**), books (cross-reference to **C9.5**), role-play (cross-reference to **C4.3** and **C9.3**) and interest table (cross-reference to **C8.5**). 'Play dough recipes' and 'Play activities' photocopiable sheets on pages 126 and 135.

Preparation

Plan the activity using the 'Activity preparation' photocopiable sheet on page 121. Ask your setting supervisor for support in doing this if necessary. Collect all the resources before the parents arrive. Photocopy the 'Play dough recipes' and 'Play activities' sheets. Make the play dough. Set up the activities in the designated areas unless you are doing this with the children.

What to do

➤ Make the setting look as welcoming as possible.

➤ Suggest that practitioners are strategically placed around the room and nominated to supervise certain activities.

➤ Welcome the parents and introduce them to the activities.

➤ Encourage the parents to circulate around all the activities, so they can 'taste' them all.

➤ As they are working with the children, make the parents aware of activities their child particularly enjoys and what they have achieved.

➤ Show the parents any displays featuring their children's work.

➤ Offer different-coloured play dough and suggest making interesting impressions with household items, such as keys, forks and pencils.

➤ Give the parents a copy of the 'Play dough recipes' sheet to try at home.

➤ Set up the book corner with chairs, cushions, bean bags and a carpet for reading and story telling.

➤ Organise the role-play area into something the parents may not have thought of, such as a travel agent or dentist's surgery.

➤ When planning the session, ask the parents to bring in interesting items from home. You can suggest a theme, such as colour, shapes, natural materials or food. Sit at a table and discuss the items with the children. Ask the children to draw a picture or write a poem or story inspired by the theme and items, and display these on the interest table.

➤ Use the 'Play activities' sheet to discuss the various options with the parents.

➤ Thank the parents for coming in and invite them to attend on another occasion.

➤ Clear away the activities and tidy up.

Tip

➤ All parents are different, so family backgrounds, values and practices will vary. As a practitioner you will need to treat parents as individuals.

P1.2: 1

Gaining your NVQ Level 2 in Early Years Care and Education *early years* **training & management**

Support and extension
Explain to the parents how you can simplify the activities to accommodate children of different developmental levels. Give them ideas for doing these activities at home. Let the parents have the photocopiable sheets to take home with them.

Evaluation
Were you well prepared before the parents arrived? Did you feel confident in sharing the activities with them? Was it helpful to have a handout for discussion? Did the parents welcome having a photocopiable sheet to take home with them?

Supporting activity
Collect other handouts that may be useful to give to parents on future occasions.

Case study
➤ At your setting you are known to work well with younger children, particularly in relation to potty training. Ali has recently shown an interest, joining in with the 'potty round'. You feel it is important to share this information with his parents. What should you discuss with them regarding Ali's future care? Write down the case study with your responses for your portfolio.

P1.2: 1, 2, 3, 4 ◄

Follow on
➤ For a specified age range, identify common milestones, such as walking, talking, teething and potty training, to inform future discussions with parents.

Cross-reference to **C1** ◄

Questions
(See answer pointers at end of chapter.)

➤ **4.** In which areas of the children's physical care should you take particular · · · · · ***P1.2***: 2 ◄
notice of parents' wishes? How should you respond to the parents?

➤ **5.** When parents express concerns about their children, how should you act · · · · ***P1.2***: 5 ◄
and whom will you tell?

➤ **6.** How can you encourage parents of children new to the setting to stay until · · ***P1.2***: 6 ◄
their child has settled?

Record the questions and your full answers and share these with your assessor.

Did you know?
Research from the Department for Education and Skills (*Researching Effective Pedagogy in the Early Years*, DfES, 2002) shows that parents feel that settings that are sensitive, responsive and consistent are more effective. This also links with other research demonstrating good practice.

Extra idea
➤ Find out if your setting has a settling-in policy. If not, try writing the key factors · · ***P1.2***: 6 ◄
you think should be included. With their permission, observe a parent and child, who are new to the setting, over a few days and write up your observations. Make comments on your observations in relation to the policy.

Practical ways of collecting evidence
Over a period of time, keep notes of any activities, communications or direct contact with parents that you have. Make notes consecutively to photocopy and

put in your portfolio. Parents may wish to give verbal or written comments on your work, on help required with their children or thanks for their care. Keep any notes or records. It may be appropriate for parents to complete a witness testimony form for you to include in your portfolio.

Check your progress

Your assessor may not directly observe you for this Unit, although where your assessor is present when you have any communication with parents this can be included. Evidence of your performance can be authenticated by witness testimonies from colleagues. Other forms of evidence include work products, such as information given and received from parents, notes of parents' concerns, your understanding of policies and procedures in relation to settling in, partnership with parents, confidentiality, accidents and child protection. You can write reflective accounts of your own practice in working with parents, giving information, developing relationships and sharing care. Other records, such as diaries, work programmes of activities highlighting where parents can be involved, child observations and children's developmental records can also be included. Due to the difficulties of collecting evidence from direct observations with parents, you may need to take part in simulation exercises, role-play or skill rehearsals.

Answer pointers

Ensure your answers are fully made for your assessor.
1. Mr. Mrs. Ms. Dr. First name. Cultural name, such as Mrs Kaur or Mr Singh. Nickname. Religious name. Personal name.
2. Talk. Notes. Setting-home link book. Diary. Noticeboards. Photographs. Displays. Videos.
3. Show. Share. Take home. Display. Invite in. Special events.
4. Listen carefully. Accommodate views. Vary sleep patterns. Special diets. Use of nappy cream. Sun lotion. Potty training.
5. Give attention. Listening skills. Open-ended questions. Calm. Undistracted. Receptive. Responsive. Reflective. Senior officer.
6. Welcome. Acceptable. Until settled. Security. Others stay. Know routine. Settle quicker. Less distressing. Meet staff. Get to know key worker.

Further information

Curriculum Guidance for the Foundation Stage
(DfEE, 2000)

Researching Effective Pedagogy in the Early Years
(DfES, 2002)

Managing to Change – Module 3 Partnership with Parents
Liz Cowley
(National Children's Bureau, 1995)

For toy libraries visit **www.natll.org.uk**

C12 Feed babies

This Unit focuses on preparing feeds and the feeding of babies between the age of six weeks and 12 months. Parents' wishes are considered and accommodated with regard to formula feed and weaning, including cultural variations. Areas covered include sterilising of equipment, making up feeds, introducing solids and feeding older babies. This Unit is appropriate for practitioners in all types of settings where babies are cared for individually or in groups.

This chapter will enable you to:
C12.1 Prepare equipment and formula feed
C12.2 Feed babies by bottle
C12.3 Prepare food and feed babies.

Element C12.1 Prepare equipment and formula feed

➤ Your assessor can observe and question you. · ◀ ***C12.1**: Range 1a, b, c, 2a, b*

Writing the rules

In the interests of efficiency, health, hygiene, consistency and good working practice, the baby food preparation area (referred to here as baby kitchen) should follow a set of basic rules. From the points identified here, draw up a sample set of rules, adding details where appropriate, for the baby kitchen with which you are familiar.
Number of babies: for all babies.

Resources

Baby kitchen; feeding and sterilising equipment; cleaning materials; computer; A4 paper; printer.

Preparation

Ask your setting supervisor for support in planning this activity if necessary.

What to do

➤ Print out these rules to display on the baby kitchen wall:
 ♦ Wash your hands.
 ♦ Ensure all surface areas are kept clean at all times.
 ♦ Wash bottles and teats in detergent, using a bottle brush and rinse under running water.
 ♦ Prepare steriliser.
 ♦ Place equipment in the sterilising solution.
 ♦ Wash your hands.
 ♦ Boil fresh water and allow to cool.
 ♦ Check formula, including the best-before date.
 ♦ Read the instructions on the packet.

✔ Tip

➤ Check there are no air bubbles inside the bottles while sterilising, and that caps and teats are fully submerged.

C12.1: 2

➤ There is no need to rinse bottles when they come out of a chemical steriliser.

C12.1: 2

- ◆ Clean and disinfect surface areas.
- ◆ Wash your hands.
- ◆ Remove the bottles and knife from the steriliser.
- ◆ Prepare formula feed strictly according to instructions.
- ◆ Add teats and caps.
- ◆ Cool quickly and keep in the fridge.
- ◆ Return milk powder and tidy kitchen.

Support and extension

In your rules, be specific about the equipment and type of sterilisation process used in your setting. There may be other steps you need to add.

Evaluation

Could you relate the exercise to your setting? Did you add additional instructions to cover all the aspects? Did you describe how to make up the formula? Were you able to print the instructions to display? Did it give you confidence to follow the process through?

Supporting activities

➤ C12.1: 2 . . . . Ask for instruction on cleaning, anti-bacterial sprays and sterilisation in the baby ◄ kitchen. Sterilisation must follow strict rules to ensure no bacteria are present that might cause infection. Find out about four different ways of sterilising bottles and teats. Write up your methods and findings, and put in your portfolio.

➤ C12.1: 7 . . . . The concentration of milk powder to water is vital. Too much can harm the baby ◄ and too little can mean the baby does not get enough nutrition. Practise measuring the formula milk under supervision.

Case study

➤ C12.1: 1, 2, 4, 8 . . . You have been asked to give the baby kitchen a spring clean and feel it would ◄ benefit from being reorganised. List the items you expect to find in a baby kitchen and draw up a plan of where you will put the different pieces of equipment and requirements for feeding babies, to provide an efficient preparation area. Take into account hygiene, storage and the need to clean bottles and sterilise. Write down the case study with your responses for your portfolio.

Follow on

➤ C12.1: 2, 4 . . . . . . Research the implications of using a microwave in the baby kitchen. In certain ◄ situations they can be dangerous. You need to know what to avoid. Discuss with your assessor the pros and cons of using a microwave for sterilising, heating milk and heating food.

Questions

(See answer pointers at end of chapter.)

➤ C12.1: 4, 7, 8 . . . . . **1.** How should milk and milk powders be used and stored? ◄

➤ C12.1: 5 . . . . **2.** What is the formula used to calculate how much milk a baby should be given ◄ over a 24-hour period?

➤ C12.1: 6 . . . . **3.** Can you identify the milk formulas for babies under 12 months old, and those ◄ that are not appropriate, according to medical advice and parental wishes?

Record the questions and your full answers and share these with your assessor.

Did you know?
Babies born between June and August tend to be smaller than average, while those born between March and May tend to be larger.

Extra idea
➤ Cut out pictures from a catalogue of feeding equipment for babies aged six · · · · *C12.1*: 1, 2 ◄
weeks to 12 months. Stick to an A4 sheet and add your comments on their suitability for developmental levels and how to clean and sterilise them. Put in your portfolio.

Element C12.2   Feed babies by bottle

➤ The assessor will need to observe you feeding the babies and question you. · · · · *Cross-reference to C13* ◄
The suggestions given here are appropriate to the interaction after the baby has   *C12.2*: range 2a, b, c
been fed.

Feeding and post-feeding play
Number of babies: individuals.

Resources
Feed; baby toys; books.

Preparation
Gather everything you will need before picking the baby up. Wash your hands. Prepare fresh feed or collect pre-prepared feed from the fridge. Check it is labelled with the baby's name.

What to do
➤ Warm the bottle of feed to the correct temperature.
➤ Check whether the baby's nappy needs changing and make sure that they are comfortable.
➤ Wash your hands.
➤ Sit in a comfortable position with the baby on your lap.
➤ Talk gently, cuddle and make eye contact.
➤ Feed, wind and wipe the baby's face.
➤ When satisfied with the feed the baby may be sleepy or ready to go and play.

Tip

➤ Between feeds encourage babies to drink plain boiled water that has cooled, especially in hot weather.

➤ When feeding, cuddle, make eye contact and talk gently to babies.

C12.2: 8

Be guided by an individual child's appetite – some like small, frequent feeds and others prefer larger, less frequent feeds.

➤ Change the baby's nappy again if required and wash your hands.

➤ Continue comforting the baby and playing gentle games, such as peep-po, looking in a mirror; using a glove puppet; shaking a rattle and looking at books. Continue a running conversation, describing what you are playing with and what you are doing.

Support and extension

Use safe materials from around the setting to offer different experiences for the baby. Use the 'Baby games' photocopiable sheet on page 136 for further ideas.

Evaluation

Did you feel confident in feeding, playing and talking to the baby? What other things can you play with? Do different babies like different toys? Do babies of different ages play with things differently? How can you improve on this activity? Do you need to ask advice of anyone?

Supporting activity

Make a list, with notes, of simple games to play with babies. Put in your portfolio.

➤ **C12.2**: *1, 4, 5, 7, 8, 10, 11*

Case study

Adam has never been a good feeder. This is one of the reasons his parents decided to bring him to the setting. His mother was becoming upset at the time it was taking – she seemed to do nothing else. What could be the reasons for Adam not feeding well? Suggest strategies to overcome these difficulties? Write down the case study with your responses for your portfolio.

➤ **C12.2**: *10*

Follow on

Find out what the alternatives are if a baby is allergic to cows' milk.

Questions

(See answer pointers at end of chapter.)

➤ **C12.2**: *3* **4.** *What equipment should you lay out prior to feeding a baby?*

➤ **C12.2**: *6* **5.** *How can you make a quick temperature check and check the rate of flow of the feed, to ensure it is safe for the individual baby?*

➤ **C12.2**: *10* **6.** *If you experienced feeding difficulties with a baby, where can you expect to find help and advice?*

Record the questions and your full answers and share these with your assessor.

Did you know?

'Babies are born with tastebuds on the roof of the mouth, walls of the throat and insides of the cheeks, as well as the tongue. Every taste is a sensation explosion. Initially, this heightened awareness directs the infant towards the sweetness of his mother's milk, imbued with the flavours of the food she is eating. Later, it will lead the child towards an eager anticipation of his local diet.' *Baby Wisdom* by Deborah Jackson (Hodder & Stoughton, 2002).

Extra idea

➤ **C12.2**: *12* Photocopy records on baby feeds that you have given and put in your portfolio.

Element C12.3   Prepare food and feed babies

➤ Your assessor can observe and question you. · · · · · · · · · · · · · · · · · ◀ **C12.3**: Range 1a, b, c, 2a, b, 3a, b ◀

Preparing baby food
Number of babies: one or more.

Resources
Food; chopping boards; implements; saucepans; serving dishes; baby dishes; spoons; anti-bacterial spray.

Preparation
Clean the kitchen area with anti-bacterial spray. Prepare the food following the recipe or instructions. Ask your supervisor for advice. Check for allergies and dietary requirements.

What to do
➤ Demonstrate your ability to prepare food for babies at different stages in the weaning and feeding process.
➤ Start with finely sieved food, move on to mashed food and increasingly solid food. When the babies have mastered the technique of swallowing without choking and are anxious to gain their independence, you can cut up pieces of food for them to pick up.
➤ Purée fruit and vegetables by rubbing through a sieve, blending or liquidising a large amount.
➤ Mash food with a fork or a potato masher. Try bananas, potatoes and cooked carrots and parsnips mashed together with a little milk.
➤ Chop vegetables and serve with minced meat and gravy.
➤ Prepare finger food suitable for older babies, such as cheese sticks, strips of chapatti, toast fingers, cucumber sticks, sliced kiwi fruit, lengths of banana and sections of peeled apple.
➤ Offer healthy snacks of melon, cooked carrot sticks with cheese sauce, fromage frais, yoghurt or a bowl of breakfast cereal, with pieces that can be picked up.
➤ Always be aware of dietary requirements as requested by the family.

Support and extension
Babies should not be weaned before they are at least four months old; some people suggest to wait until six months. Wait for the babies to indicate with actions that they are ready for solid food. You need to be aware of an individual baby's readiness for particular types of food.

✔ **Tip**
➤ Babies do not need teeth to bite and chew, as their gums are strong and hard enough to cope with breadsticks, apple pieces and banana.

C13.3: 2, 5, 8

➤ It is advisable to offer babies many different tastes in the early months, although not all at the same time. It is believed they are less likely to become fussy eaters later on.

C12.3: 3

Evaluation

Did you feed different types of food to babies at different developmental levels? What did you observe? Did they all manage well? Were any babies in danger of choking? Do you know what to do if a baby does choke on a piece of food? Did the babies enjoy the food? Did they decide when they had had enough? Did you check their favourite foods with colleagues or parents? Can you offer an alternative diet, such as a vegetarian diet?

Supporting activities

Keep a weaning recipe book. Every time you come across some food or dish appropriate to this age group, make a note of it so you have a useful collection for future reference. Draw up a chart showing stages of development during the first year, to include food and feeding.

➤ **C12.3**: *1, 2, 5, 7, 8, 9*

Case study

Lily, in common with other babies her age, is testing her independence. She is ten months old and has not mastered handling cutlery, but desperately wants to feed herself. What sort of food and implements can you offer Lily that will satisfy her developmental needs and ensure she has a nutritious diet? Write down the case study with your responses for your portfolio.

➤ **C12.3**: *4* · · · · · · ·

Follow on

Assess the different forms of protective clothing and accessories available for babies. There are small terry towelling bibs, plastic-backed absorbent coveralls, flexible plastic 'pelican' bibs and plastic bibs. Which are preferable? How easy are they to put on and remove? Are they easy to clean? Do they serve the purpose?

Questions

(See answer pointers at end of chapter.)

➤ **C12.3**: *1, 3* · · · · · · **7.** *What difficulties might a baby with special needs experience during feeding?*

➤ **C12.3**: *2, 5, 7* · · · · · **8.** *What techniques can you use to encourage babies to take weaning foods?*

➤ **C12.3**: *6* · · · · · · · **9.** *How can you enhance babies' enjoyment when feeding?*

Record the questions and your full answers and share these with your assessor.

Did you know?

Babies need calcium to develop healthy bones and teeth. The body more easily absorbs calcium from dairy products than from other foods.

Extra idea

➤ **C12.3**: *7, 8* · · · · · · · Use the 'Baby menu' photocopiable sheet on page 137 to draw up a balanced diet for a nine-month-old baby. Describe the texture of the food.

Practical ways of collecting evidence

Keep a record of when you have fed the babies, how much feed they have taken and your comments on how well they fed. Note whether they were offered solid food and when it was offered, whether before, during, after or between feeds. Note the consistency and texture of the food and the babies' reaction to it at different ages. Put the records in your portfolio.

Check your progress

This is a very practical Unit and you are expected to be directly observed by your assessor for at least one aspect of each of the Range categories for all three Elements. This will involve the preparation of feeds, feeding a baby and giving food to babies under 12 months old. You are likely to cover more than one aspect, but if not, or any of the Performance Criteria are not observed, you can collect evidence by other means. You can show where feeds are prepared, including the sterilised equipment. You may rehearse the sterilisation of equipment and making up of feeds and be observed doing that. Colleagues can complete witness testimonies, feedback from parents can be recorded and used, as well as records of when you have fed the babies. Your assessor can question you on your understanding of policies on meals and feeding routines.

Answer pointers

Ensure your answers are fully made for your assessor.

1. Hygienically. Within best-before date. According to manufacturer's instructions. In original container. Lid kept on. Dry. Reconstituted. Sterilised bottles. In fridge. Mixed milk kept up to 24 hours.

2. Check with packet. 75ml/500g body weight in 24 hours. Respond to babies' needs. Judge by weight gain.

3. Baby milk formula powder. Expressed milk. Starter milk. Follow-on milk. Soya milk. Not evaporated milk, condensed milk, goats' milk, unmodified cows' milk. Medical advice.

4. Tray. Bib or soft cloth. Bottle or feed. Teat. Cap. Jug. Hot water. Tissues.

5. Body temperature. Test on inside of wrist. Comfortable. Milk drips out when held upside down.

6. Supervisor. Parent. Health Visitor. Doctor.

7. Unable to suck. Might choke. Floppy baby. Will not wake. Cleft lip and palate. May tire easily.

8. Right consistency. Temperature. Introduce gradually. Give before milk. Gain baby's interest. Give between feeds.

9. Talk to baby. Eye contact. Cuddle. Patterned dishes. Coloured spoons. Fancy bibs. Sit at the table. With other children.

Further information

The Pregnancy Book
(NHS, 2001)
www.hpe.org.uk

C13 Provide for babies' physical developmental needs

This is a basic Unit focusing on the care of babies between birth and 12 months. It includes washing and dressing babies, changing nappies and cleaning and maintaining baby clothes and nursery equipment. You will also be expected to give physical and sensory stimulation to encourage physical, social, emotional, intellectual and language development. It is appropriate for practitioners in all types of settings, both in domestic and day care provision.

This chapter will enable you to:
C13.1 Wash babies
C13.2 Change nappies and dress babies
C13.3 Encourage development through stimulation
C13.4 Clean and maintain clothing and nursery equipment.

Element C13.1   Wash babies

➤ **C3.1**: Range 1a, b · · Your assessor can observe and question you. ◀

Bath-time fun
Number of babies: individual babies.

Resources
Baby bath; towels; baby soap and lotions suitable for the baby – check for allergies; changing mat; clean clothes; wipes; clean nappy; bath toys; cotton wool; flannel; laundry bag; protective clothing.

Preparation
Ensure the bathroom is warm enough. Put warm water in the bath and have items ready in advance.

What to do
➤ Prepare a checklist of the all the items you need.
➤ Ensure you follow parental wishes and good practice, according to the setting's policies.
➤ The active function of a bath is cleanliness, so bath the baby according to procedure. However a lot of fun and learning can take place at the same time, so try some of the following ideas:
♦ Blow bubbles for the baby to catch.
♦ Pour water from one plastic tea cup to another.
♦ Squirt water with a squeezy toy or bottle.
♦ Pat and swish the water.
♦ Press a ping-pong ball under the water and watch it pop up.
♦ Pour water out of a colander.

Tip

➤ Not all babies like water. Handle them gently, distract them with toys and speak calmly but confidently.

C13.1: 10

➤ Take care not to let babies slip when bathing with soap.

C13.1: 10

early years
training &
management

➤ Dry and dress the baby and leave in a safe place while you empty the bath, remove the dirty clothes and nappy, and tidy up.

Support and extension
New babies do not need toys, but as they grow they will begin to enjoy the sensation of water as they kick and splash. When the babies can sit up they will enjoy playing for a while. Be selective, only introducing two or three toys at a time. Choose toys appropriate to the development of the child.

Evaluation
Did you feel confident when bathing the baby?

Supporting activities
Find out the correct temperatures for the bathroom and bath water. Observe others bathing babies if you have not done it before. Make yourself fully aware of the safety issues relating to bath time and discuss with your assessor.

Case study
➤ Max's mother tries her best, however each Monday morning Max arrives in a less than fresh state. She finds weekends particularly challenging, caring for Max on her own. You suspect that, other than changing his nappy and wiping his mouth, she washes neither his body nor his clothes. How can you prepare for Max's time with you and what practical steps can you take to ensure his comfort and care? Write down the case study with your responses for your portfolio.

C13.1: 1, 2, 3, 5, 8, 9, ◄
11, 12, 14

Follow on
➤ Design a poster for parents giving the important points on washing, dressing and changing babies. Put in your portfolio.

Cross-reference to P1 ◄

Questions
(See answer pointers at end of chapter.)
➤ **1.** *What health and safety factors should you be aware of when bathing a baby?* · · · **C13.1**: 1, 2, 5, 6, 8, 10 ◄
➤ **2.** *You should be aware of bath-time practices from diverse ethnic and cultural* · · · **C13.1**: 4, 6 ◄
backgrounds. Describe some of these.
➤ **3.** *Describe the process of bathing a baby – where to start and in what order to* · · **C13.1**: 9 ◄
continue.

Record the questions and your full answers and share these with your assessor.

Did you know?
The word 'midwife' means 'a woman who is *with* the mother at birth'.
In France a midwife is called a 'sage-femme', which means wise woman.
The term 'man-midwife' first appeared in 1770.

➤ **C13.1**: *1, 2, 3, 5, 6,*
7, 8, 9, 12, 13, 14

Extra idea
If a baby is not having a bath at the setting, demonstrate your competence to
your assessor by washing and drying the baby's hands and face and completing a
nappy change.

Element C13.2   Change nappies and dress babies

➤ **C13.2**: *Range 1a, b*

Your assessor can observe and question you.

Sweet and clean
Number of babies: individual babies.

Resources
Clean clothes; nappy; baby wipes; nappy disposal bag; nappy cream, if used;
laundry bag; protective clothing; latex gloves, if required; changing mat; baby toys;
mobile.

Preparation
Prepare resources for nappy changing and dressing. Wash your hands and put on
protective clothing and gloves.

What to do
➤ Prepare a checklist of the all the items you need.
➤ Place the baby on the changing mat.
➤ Talk to the baby throughout the process, giving a running commentary
on what you are doing. Point out the names of things and parts of the body.
Let the baby respond.
➤ Offer the baby a selection of small toys to play with.
➤ Hang mobiles above the nappy changing area.
➤ Change the nappy according to the practices of the setting.
➤ Let the baby kick and exercise for a short time without a nappy on.
➤ Dispose of the nappy and wash your hands.
➤ Change the baby's clothes. Take your time and stay calm.
➤ Remove used clothes for laundering.
➤ Return the baby to a safe play area, tidy up and disinfect the changing area.

Support and extension
Choose toys appropriate to the development of the baby. Practise on younger
babies, as they do not crawl away, so you come up to speed for changing mobile
infants.

Evaluation
Were you comfortable carrying out these tasks? Were you aware of the health
and safety issues? Do you feel confident in your ability to change babies of
different ages? Do you understand the importance of high standards of hygiene in
the baby nursery?

Supporting activity
Investigate the disposal of nappies at your setting and what happens to them
when they leave the premises.

Tip

➤ Only use nappy creams
and wipes as directed by the
parents. Some babies may
have allergic reactions to
certain products.

C13.2: *4*

➤ Wipe a baby girl's bottom
from the front to the back to
reduce the risk of infection.
With boys do not pull their
foreskin back.

Gaining your NVQ Level 2 in Early Years Care and Education   early years
**training &
management**

Case study

➤ Darcy and Alice are twins, and their mother is very proud of them. She likes to dress them in identical clothes in pastel colours. Unfortunately one day, at lunchtime, Alice spills her chocolate blancmange on her dress and tights. How will you deal with this situation? How will you respond to Alice's personal predicament and what will you do with the clothes? Write down the case study with your responses for your portfolio.

C13.2: *1, 2, 3, 4, 5, 9, 11* ◄

Follow on

It is likely that you will care for twins at some time in your childcare career. Find out about the special circumstances regarding their care, the pleasures as well as the difficulties. Look up the Twins and Multiple Births Association website: **www.tamba.org.uk**.

Questions

(See answer pointers at end of chapter.)

➤ **4.** *What are the health and safety issues relating to changing nappies?* · · · · · · · **C13.2**: *1, 2, 6, 7, 12, 13*◄

➤ **5.** *What health and safety issues should be considered when dressing babies?* · · · · **C13.2**: *5* ◄

➤ **6.** *If you have concerns about a baby's health, what should you do and who can* · · **C13.2**: *8* ◄
you tell?

Did you know?

One in every 70 UK births are twins. Two thirds are non-identical (the babies grow from two separate fertilised eggs); one third are identical (a single fertilised egg splits in two). Identical twins are always the same sex and identical twin births occur randomly in the population. Non-identical twins often run in families. They can consist of either sex and are no more likely to look alike or share common characteristics than other siblings.

Extra idea

➤ Find out about different types of nappies. Look into the different qualities of · · · **C13.2**: *5* ◄
disposable nappies, terry towelling nappies and environmentally-friendly nappies. For information visit the website: **www.wen.org.uk**.

Element C13.3 Encourage development through stimulation

➤ Your assessor can observe and question you. · · · · · · · · · · · · · · · · · · **C13.3**: *Range 1a, b* ◄

Baby playtime

Number of babies: all babies.

Resources

Variety of toys and materials.

Preparation

Where appropriate, plan the activity using the 'Activity preparation' photocopiable sheet on page 121. Ask your setting supervisor for support in doing this if necessary. Check that all toys and materials are safe and suitable for the developmental level of the babies. Ensure there is a clear, safe play space available. If outdoors, check the area for potential hazards.

What to do

➤ Put small toys inside and outside a small cardboard box for babies to explore.
➤ Place a large cardboard box on its side for the babies to climb in and out of.
➤ Fill a paper bag with scrunched paper and stick down the top. Press the corners in to make a ball to roll back and forth.
➤ Build a tower of bricks.
➤ Sing nursery rhymes while bouncing the baby on your knee.
➤ Play music and support the baby, letting them sway to the music.
➤ Fill a basket with objects from around the setting. Encourage the babies to explore the objects, taking them out of the basket and putting them back again.
➤ Make a shaker by putting lentils in a container and taping the lid down firmly.
➤ Allow the babies to bang a saucepan with a wooden spoon.

Support and extension

Provide toys appropriate to the developmental level of the babies. Check the recommended age for commercial toys.

✔ **Tip**

➤ Pulling faces, cuddling, smiling, tickling, stroking, bouncing and massaging are all forms of communication.

C13.3: 3, 4

Evaluation

If you showed the baby how to do something, such as putting items in and out of a box, did they copy you?

Supporting activity

Closely observe a baby at play. Babies learn so much so fast. Note the exploration and discovery, the repetition and learning, how independent they are and how much they want adults to participate. Record your findings for your portfolio.

➤ **C13.3**: 1, 2, 3, 4, 5, · · ·
6, 7, 8, 9

Case study

Amelia, at 11 months, is a placid baby. She does not appear to be very inquisitive and will sit and observe the activities around her for long periods of time if left to her own devices. Her mother is disabled and not very mobile. She does not encourage Amelia to move around very much. How can you stimulate Amelia to encourage her to explore within the limits of her family situation? Write down the case study with your responses for your portfolio.

Follow on

Explore the difficulties that disabled parents may experience in bringing up their children. Talk to your colleagues and other professionals.

Questions

(See answer pointers at end of chapter.)

➤ **C13.3**: 1, 2, 6 · · · · · · **7.** *How can you provide a stimulating indoor environment for babies between birth and 12 months?*

➤ **8.** *How and when, in the routine, can you encourage interaction and* · · · · · · · · **C13.3**: *4* ◄
communication to stimulate a baby's development?

➤ **9.** *What baby safety equipment would you expect to see in a birth-to-two setting?* · · **C13.3**: *8* ◄

Record the questions and your full answers and share these with your assessor.

Did you know?
Nine out of ten babies that are born deaf are born to hearing parents. British Sign Language is recognised by the European Parliament as a minority language. Sign language is a form of visual communication that has its own grammar, structure and word order.

Extra ideas

➤ Suggest ways to stimulate a baby outdoors, such as a walk, sitting outside in · · · · **C13.3**: *1, 2, 7* ◄
the pram and playing outside.

➤ When babies have mastered new skills, such as clapping, share with the parents. · · **C13.3**: *9, cross-reference to* **P1** ◄

Element C13.4 Clean and maintain clothing and nursery equipment

➤ Your assessor can observe and question you. · **C13.4**: *Range 1a, c, 2a, b* ◄

Maintain a baby nursery
Number of babies: for whole group.

Resources
Cleaning materials; clean cloths; bucket or bowl; laundry bag; clean bed linen; protective clothing; latex gloves, if used.

Preparation
Collect resources together, out of the babies' reach.

What to do
➤ Choose a time when you can work undisturbed, when the babies are out of the room.
➤ Put on protective clothing and gloves, if used.
➤ Strip the cots, placing the dirty linen in the laundry bag.
➤ Clean and dry the mattresses and cots according to setting's procedures. Leave to air before replacing the bed linen.
➤ Wipe clean prams, buggies, playpens, high chairs and bouncing cradles.
➤ Thoroughly clean the changing mat and nappy changing area.
➤ Wash the machine washable soft toys, rag books or baby mats with an appropriate wash cycle, hang to dry and thoroughly air.
➤ Clean the toys with soapy water or anti-bacterial spray.
➤ Put away all the cleaning materials.

Support and extension
Use the 'Equipment checklist' photocopiable sheet on page 138 to ensure routine maintenance is conducted according to procedural guidelines. Fill in the blank boxes with relevant equipment from your setting.

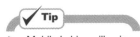 **Tip**

➤ Mobile babies will enjoy copying you. Let the babies help with domestic chores, such as dusting and sweeping.

➤ Cot bumpers are not advisable for babies as they may snuggle against them while sleeping and overheat. Similarly, duvets should not be used, because a baby's temperature control is not well developed.

Evaluation

Are you familiar with the setting's cleaning and maintenance procedures? How often are the different items cleaned and checked? Which cleaning materials should you use for which purpose? Where are they stored?

Supporting activities

Find out the effects of washing baby clothes in randomly selected washing powders and liquids. Show your assessor where needles and thread are kept for stitching buttons on.

➤ **C13.4**: *1, 2, 3, 4,* · · · ·
5, 6

Case study

During the morning Kiana has shown signs of illness. She has become hot and fretful, refused any drinks and vomited in her cot. Her father has been called. Her key worker has sponged her with tepid water, comforted her and changed her clothes. You remove the worst of the vomit and, to ensure infection is not spread around the setting, you organise the cleaning process. Describe how you will undertake this task. Write down the case study with your responses for your portfolio.

➤ **C13.4**: *6, cross-* · · · ·
reference to **E1**

Follow on

Find out what cleaning materials and washing products are in use in the setting. Check how they should be stored and used.

Questions

(See answer pointers at end of chapter.)

➤ **C13.4**: *1* · · · · · · · · **10.** *Can you describe how to remove, sluice and disinfect soiled baby linen, and explain what you would do with it?*

➤ **C13.4**: *1, 2, 6* · · · · · **11.** *Why is it important to clean and disinfect baby clothes and nursery equipment?*

➤ **C13.4**: *7* · · · · · · · · **12.** *What sort of repairs to baby clothes and equipment fall within your role in the setting? What will you do with something outside of your responsibility?*

Record the questions and your full answers and share these with your assessor.

Did you know?

Every year nearly 800,000 children under the age of five visit hospital as the result of an accident.

Extra idea

➤ **C13.4**: *1, 6* · · · · · · Using the 'Spider chart' photocopiable sheet on page 122, write 'Routine cleaning and maintenance' in the centre. In each surrounding box identify an item, how it is maintained and how often it is cleaned or checked.

Practical ways of collecting evidence

The first three Elements are all integral to the regular routine and are likely to be directly observed by your assessor. For the fourth Element your assessor can be given a tour of the setting and shown the laundry area, storage for cleaning materials, nappy changing area, where washing and bathing takes place, and the play area. You can be questioned on all of these areas.

Check your progress

You are expected to be directly observed by your assessor for at least one aspect of each Range category for each of the four Elements. You can be observed for more if this is practical. Some Performance Criteria are not likely to be seen and for this you will need to provide different types of evidence. Your assessor can inspect the setting and discuss with you the area of your responsibility for cleaning and maintenance. You can write reflective accounts of your performance, including diagrams or photographs of home-made play materials, log books, plans for play activities and routine maintenance, baby observations, witness testimonies from colleagues and reports by you, or in which you have been mentioned.

Answer pointers

Ensure your answers are fully made for your assessor.

1. Room temperature. Water temperature. Do not leave unattended. Cover taps. Nothing breakable in water. Support baby. Change on firm surface. Cold water before hot. Hygienic. Clean. No baby powder. Reduce cross infection. Allergies.

2. Plaited hair. Circumcision. Coconut oil for dry skin. Special shampoos. Massage oil. Skin preparations. Shaved head.

3. Body. Clean eyes. Nappy area. Face. Hair. (Consider the order.)

4. Falling from changing trolley. Washing hands. Disposal of nappies. Wearing protective aprons. Wearing gloves. Grabbing slipping baby may break limb. Disinfecting area.

5. Avoid ties. Loose buttons. Toggles on neck strings. Flouncy dresses for crawling. Access to nappy area. Ribbons. Warm. Not overheated.

6. Identify baby's condition. Report immediately. Seek advice. Refer to supervisor. Tell parents.

7. Mobiles. Bright displays. Toys. Mirrors. Different textures. Books. Pictures.

8. Talking. Singing. Playing. Cuddling. Play time. Nappy changing time. Bath time. Feeding. Whispering. Making sounds.

9. Socket covers. Fireguards. Reins. High-chair straps. Harness.

10. Laundry bucket. Rinse excess off. Soak in nappy sterilising fluid. Wash in machine. Dry. Air.

11. Cross infection. Low resistance. Everything in mouth. Vulnerable.

12. Minor sewing. Report to senior colleague. Tighten screws. Emergency repairs.

Further information

From Birth to Five Years, Children's Developmental Progress
Mary D Sheridan
(Routledge, 1997)

Birth to Five
(Health Promotion, 1999)

M1 Monitor, store and prepare materials and equipment

This Unit looks into giving administrative and technical support on request. It includes setting up technical equipment for use by others. Also included is photocopying, preparing art and craft materials, other play and learning materials and the monitoring of stock levels, such as stationery, play and cleaning materials.

This chapter will enable you to:
M1.1 Prepare equipment
M1.2 Prepare materials
M1.3 Monitor and store materials.

Element M1.1 Prepare equipment

➤ **M1.1**: Range 1b · · · · · Your assessor can observe and question you. ◄

The cinema
Number of children: four.

Resources
Video player; television; two entertainment videos; four chairs; tray; popcorn; clean, empty yoghurt pots; popping corn or microwavable popcorn; cooking facilities; spoon; small table; play money; cash box; cardboard tube; Cellophane; small sheets of card; paper; felt-tipped pens; screen; curtains.

Preparation
Plan the activity using the 'Activity preparation' photocopiable sheet on page 121. Ask your setting supervisor for support in doing this if necessary. Check for allergies and dietary requirements. Choose a dark corner in which to arrange the imaginative play area as a cinema. Set out the television, video player and the chairs in two rows facing the television. Stand the small table by the entrance. If possible, screen the area off from the rest of the room and draw the curtains or black out the windows.

What to do
➤ Explain to the children that they are going to the cinema, but first they have to get ready for it.

➤ Can the children suggest what they need to get into the cinema and what they would need inside, such as tickets, someone selling tickets, someone to show them where to sit and popcorn.

➤ Let the children choose which activity to prepare.

➤ Provide felt-tipped pens and card for one child to make the tickets.

➤ Give one child the toy money and cash box to set up the booking office on the small table.

➤ Let one child decorate the cardboard tube with felt-tipped pens then scrunch Cellophane into the end to make a torch.

➤ Nominate one child to set out the yoghurt pots on the tray ready for the popcorn.

➤ Wash your hands and make the popcorn according to the instructions on the packet.

➤ If the children are present when you cook the corn, encourage them to listen to the corn popping. Take great care as cookers, utensils and popcorn will all be very hot initially.

➤ Allow to cool and spoon the cooked popcorn into the yoghurt pots.

➤ Let the children choose a role, whether working in the booking office, showing people to their seats with a torch, selling popcorn or as a customer. Let them swap roles.

➤ Let the children act out the roles, choose which video to watch and settle down to watch.

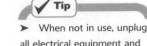

Tip

➤ When not in use, unplug all electrical equipment and use a socket cover.

Support and extension

➤ Cut out ready-made tickets and money from the 'Cinema role-play' · · · · · · · · · *Cross-reference to* **C9** ◄
photocopiable sheet on page 139 for younger children to use. Challenge older children to suggest additional features for the cinema.

Evaluation

Were you confident setting up the video player and television set? Did you make all the safety checks? Was the electrical equipment in a safe place where it would not be knocked or damaged? Were the children present when you cooked the popcorn? Is this advisable? Will you do this activity again? What changes will you make and why? Did the children enjoy the role-play?

Supporting activity

Use torches for a 'light' theme activity. Investigate objects in cupboards, storerooms and dark corners. Check that torches work, where replacement batteries can found and show the children how to use them. Discuss the hazardous nature of batteries and how they should be disposed of.

Case study

➤ You have been delegated to prepare banners, signs and notices for a fundraising event in four weeks. You would also like to develop your IT skills and this will give you the opportunity to gain more practical experience. Describe how you will set about the task, what resources you need, what checks you need to make and how you will prepare the banners, signs and notices. Write down the case study with your responses for your portfolio.

M1.1: 1, 2, 3, 4, 5, 6, 7 ◄

Follow on

Develop your IT skills, as they are valuable and useful in childcare and early years work.

Questions

(See answer pointers at end of chapter.)

➤ **M1.1**: 1 . . . . **1.** Why is it important to follow the manufacturer's instructions when preparing to ◄ use equipment?

➤ **M1.1**: 3 . . . . **2.** What are the health and safety requirements of a range of audio, visual and ◄ computer equipment in your setting?

➤ **M1.1**: 6 . . . . **3.** Why should you always report faults in equipment to the relevant person in your ◄ setting?

Record the questions and your full answers and share these with your assessor.

Did you know?

A competent electrician should check electrical appliances at least once a year. Records should be kept on equipment used and the checks made.

Extra idea

➤ **M1.1**: 1, 2, 3 . . . . . Check if your setting has a policy on inspecting and using electrical equipment. If ◄ not, write your own, suggesting the guidance you believe should be included, such as health and safety requirements, positioning of equipment, where instructions and accessories are kept and who to report faults to. Put in your portfolio.

Element M1.2   Prepare materials

➤ **M1.2**: Range 1a, ... Your assessor can observe and question you. ◄
2a, b

Make a greeting card

Number of children: six.

Resources

Six card copies of 'Greeting card' photocopiable sheet on page 140; choice of craft materials for decoration; glue, if required.

Preparation

Plan the activity using the 'Activity preparation' photocopiable sheet on page 121. Ask your setting supervisor for support in doing this if necessary. Put materials in separate containers ready for use.

What to do

➤ Give the children a 'Greeting card' sheet each and show them how to fold the paper to make a four-fold card. Fold the sheet across the centre, from top to bottom, with the design on the outside. Fold a second time so the blank rectangle falls on the inside. The card should have the design on the front and 'Made especially for you by:' on the back.

➤ Encourage the children to write a message and signature inside the card and their name on the back.

➤ Offer the children a selection of ways to decorate the card, such as ink stampers; stickers; glitter; stars and sequins; finger prints; felt-tipped pens; cut-outs from old Christmas cards.

Support and extension
Help younger children fold their card and scribe a message for them. Let them make their own marks for their name. Offer older children finer decorative materials.

Tip

➤ Your health and safety is just as important as the children's. Take care when preparing materials and using guillotines, craft knives and sharp scissors.

M1.2: 4

Evaluation
Did you have trouble making card copies of the sheet? Did you find enough appropriate materials to make attractive cards? Did you allow the children choice in design and decoration? Did you only help when it was requested or needed? What did the children learn from the activity? What did you learn?

Supporting activity
➤ Practise using the photocopier to its full extent. Give examples of single-sided · · · **M1.2**: *1, 2, 4* ◄
copying, double-sided copying, reducing images, enlarging images and collating copies ('collating' ensures several copies of a few pages are gathered in order; some photocopiers can also staple sheets together).

Case study
➤ Next week two members of staff are on holiday, leaving the setting with the **M1.2**: *3, 4, 6, 7, 8* ◄
minimum staffing ratio. The weekly plan has been produced and it includes a number of activities requiring an assortment of materials. You are asked to make some preparations while you have time and store them in the cupboard. What sort of things can be prepared in advance and how will you ensure everyone knows what they are for? Write down the case study with your responses for your portfolio.

Follow on
Consider how much advance preparation you can do on a regular basis. It can be more efficient to prepare all the photocopying, for example, for the day or week. This will reduce the need to visit the photocopier several times a day and wait for it to warm up each time.

Questions
(See answer pointers at end of chapter.)
➤ **4.** *How can you gauge the amount of paper and materials you will need for the* · · **M1.2**: *1, 8* ◄
activities?
➤ **5.** *What are the health and safety considerations related to paper, art and craft* · · **M1.2**: *3* ◄
materials, play materials and learning materials?
➤ **6.** *If you find faults and shortages in equipment and materials, what should you* · · · **M1.2**: *5, 6* ◄
do with the information?

Record the questions and your full answers and share these with your assessor.

Did you know?
In their book, *Tender Care and Early Learning* (High Scope Press, 2000), Jacalyn Post and Mary Hohmann emphasise the need to give young children choices. They say that while they do not have a choice as to whether they go to childcare settings, 'each part of the day, however, presents opportunities for choices and decisions they *can* make ... what to hold, look at, or whether, how and how long to participate in an activity.'.

➤ **M1.2**: 1, 2, 3 · · · · · ·

Extra idea
If you do not have a photocopier in your setting your assessor may be able to ◄
observe you in the library or NVQ assessment centre.

Element M1.3 Monitor and store materials

➤ **M1.3**: Range 1a, b, · · ·
c, d

Your assessor can observe and question you. ◄

Labelling materials

Resources
A3 card; scissors; Blu-Tack; laminator (optional).

Preparation
Agree any special arrangements with your supervisor for organising the storage
of materials. Use the A3 card to create labels for: 'Decorations', 'Sugar paper',
'Card', 'Glue', Paint', Decorative paper', 'Frieze paper', and 'Assorted paper'. Cut
out individual labels and laminate, if desired.

What to do
➤ Assess the current storage situation
for art and craft materials, papers and play
materials.
➤ Draw up a shelf plan to make the most
efficient use of the space.
➤ Ensure the most frequently used items
are the most easily accessible.
➤ Follow health and safety regulations,
such as storing heavy items lower down.
➤ Remove items from the storage area
with care.
➤ Sort small items into plastic or
cardboard boxes, cleaning when
necessary.
➤ Remove any damaged or deteriorating
materials and report to the relevant
person.
➤ Clean shelves and ensure they are fully dry before replacing items.
➤ Place materials neatly in revised positions.
➤ Blu-Tack labels to boxes or shelves.
➤ Draw a diagram of the storage area or cupboard shelves, labelling the
contents of each shelf, to enable all staff to locate materials. Display by the area.

Support and extension

➤ Cross-reference to · · ·
E2

Due to time constraints and the particular situation, it may be necessary to ◄
reorganise the stock in stages, one cupboard at a time. With large storage areas
and stocks it can be beneficial to work with a colleague.

Evaluation
Did you find the task daunting at first? Do you feel you made a good choice for
the reorganisation? In retrospect, should you have organised things differently?

Did you complete the task within the given timescale? If not, why not? Did you feel a sense of achievement on the completion of the task?

Supporting activity

As you replace materials, note the amounts remaining of each for monitoring purposes. Report findings to the relevant person, making suggestions for additional stock where appropriate. Agree a period for rechecking and reordering the stock materials.

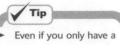

> **Tip**
>
> ➤ Even if you only have a small amount of materials in your setting, it is important for you to store them effectively.

M1.3: 1

Case study

➤ You are on duty when a delivery of art and craft materials is made. You are asked to unpack it and put away it in the appropriate place. When you go to the store cupboard you find it in a muddle and do not know where to put the new items. How will you deal with this situation in a tactful way, in order to maintain good working relationships with your colleagues? Write down the case study with your responses for your portfolio.

M1.3: 1, 3, 4, 5, cross- ◄
reference to *CU10*

Follow on

➤ Encourage the children to pack materials away after use in the designated drawers, boxes and shelves. Knowing where to find materials makes for a more effective environment, is less frustrating and gives the children a sense of pride in their environment.

M1.3: 1   ◄

Questions

(See answer pointers at end of chapter.)

➤ **7.** *How should the following art, craft and play materials be stored: paper, glue,* · · ·   *M1.3*: 1   ◄
paint, play dough and sand?

➤ **8.** *Why is it important to monitor the storage and use of any materials in the* · · · · *M1.3*: 3, 4, 5, 6, 7   ◄
setting?

➤ **9.** *What health and safety considerations do you need to make for your personal* · · *M1.3*: 8   ◄
safety when moving and reorganising paper, art and craft materials and play materials?

Record the questions and your full answers and share these with your assessor.

Did you know?

The Chinese invented paper making about 2000 years ago. Egyptian paper, made from papyrus, was in general use in Europe until the 8th or 9th century, when it was slowly replaced by paper made from cotton – a skill learned by the Arabs from the Chinese. Today's paper is largely made from wood pulp.

Extra ideas

➤ Make a checklist of the stocks of materials in your setting. Indicate where stocks · · *M1.3*: 6, 7   ◄
are low and may need reordering.

Practical ways of collecting evidence

There are many occasions throughout this book when suggestions have been made for preparing materials and photocopying activity sheets. Your assessor will have observed some of these. There is no need to repeat the exercise specifically for this Element as it can be cross-referenced to **M1**. Look back through previous direct observation records for evidence.

Check your progress

Much of this Unit is very practical and your assessor will directly observe you. You must be observed for at least one aspect of each Range statement for each of the three Elements. If some of the Performance Criteria and Range categories are not covered by direct observation you must provide alternative forms of evidence. Evidence can be gained from work products, such as notes on instructions given on the preparation of equipment, papers you have copied, records of materials used and a checklist of materials. You can include reflective accounts of your performance undertaking the relevant tasks, plans showing preparation of activities and witness testimonies.

Answer pointers

Ensure your answers are fully made for your assessor.

1. Safety. Prevent damage. Correctly positioned. Correct fuse. Reduce harm.

2. No frayed leads. Overloaded sockets. Balanced safely. Eye strain. Burns. Over heating.

3. Prevent accident. Initiate repair. Arrange inspection. Record fault. Reduce frustration.

4. Instructed. Number of children. Experience. Try it out. Previous usage. Stock records.

5. Suitable for purpose. Stored correctly. Weight. In original containers. Safe. Non-toxic.

6. Take note. Report promptly. Be accurate. Double check. Follow instruction.

7. Paper: large sheets at bottom; in sizes; flat; rolled; types together; out of sunlight. Glue: in original container; cleaned top; upright; out of sunlight. Paint: colours visible; lidded containers. Play dough: plastic lidded box; in fridge. Sand: sack or bucket; covered; sand tray.

8. Reorder. Deteriorate. Rotate. Procedures. Routine. Safety.

9. Light items on top shelf. Step ladder. Heavy items low down. Move small amounts at a time. Work in pairs. Do not take risks. Ask for advice. Do not over stretch.

Further information

Child Accident Prevention Trust, 18–20 Farringdon Lane, London EC1R 3HA
www.capt.org.uk

Tender Care and Early Learning, Supporting Families and Toddlers in Childcare Settings
Jacalyn Post and Mary Hohmann
(High Scope Press, 2000)

P9 Work with parents in a group

This Unit covers working with parents in a variety of group settings, both formal and informal. You need to be able to work with parents who are new to the group, those that are established, those from various social and cultural backgrounds and those with diverse skills and levels of confidence. You will be expected to explain different aspects of the operation of the group. You need to encourage parents and help them to participate in the differing functions of the group. The functions include management, fundraising activities, publicity, provision and maintenance of equipment and premises, social events, outings and children's activities. It is appropriate to practitioners in all types of settings where children are cared for individually or in groups.

This chapter will enable you to:
P9.1 Inform parents about the operation of the group
P9.2 Encourage parents to participate in group functions
P9.3 Encourage parents to participate in children's activities.

Element P9.1 Inform parents about the operation of the group

➤ Your assessor can observe and question you. · *P9.1*: Range 1a, b, c, d, ◄ 2a, b

Informing parents
Groups can be held for a variety of reasons. It may be a parents' evening, parent-teacher association meeting, fund-raising committee, celebration or event group, parenting group meeting, management committee, working bee (where parents help with maintenance of premises and resources), group to promote the setting, social events committee, trips and outings committee, coffee morning, activity session or to learn about what goes on in the regular routine.

Resources
Resources relevant to the information being prepared and distributed.

Preparation
Plan this with the support of your setting supervisor. Choose and prepare the most appropriate method to distribute information.

What to do
➤ Discuss the methods of communication you have decided to use with your colleagues, such as word of mouth, letter, poster, newsletter or a combination. Tell the parents. Follow it up with a letter and display a poster or refer to the meeting in the newsletter.

Tip

➤ Communication is more than written words and verbal messages. Non-verbal communication, the tone of voice used and the attitude towards others, also give a strong message to observers.

➤ Agree on the amount of information to be given in each format. It should be clear and accurate, without overloading the parent with unnecessary details, but giving enough information so they know what, where, when and why there is to be a group meeting.

➤ Consider parents for whom English is not their first language and strategies to ensure they are fully informed, such as translation, interpretation or in a written form if they can get help to read it.

➤ Consider any parents with disabilities who may find it difficult to access information, such as deaf and visually impaired parents.

➤ Think about parents who cannot read and the alternative methods to impart information to them.

➤ Ask for help from your colleagues and supervisor if you are not clear on any of the issues.

➤ Prepare the written information and check for inaccuracies or spelling mistakes.

➤ Talk to parents face to face about the group meeting.

Support and extension

Make arrangements for written information to be recorded on tape for parents who cannot read or are visually impaired. Make sure they know the information is available. Add at least a few words in heritage languages to break down barriers and show that you value all the parents and children.

Evaluation

Did you know where to start this exercise? Were you confident communicating directly with the parents? Did you ask for support and advice? Was the feedback on your performance favourable? Can you improve your communication skills?

Supporting activity

➤ *P9.1*: 1 . . . . Photocopy the blank 'Notice' photocopiable sheet on page 141. Use it to design ◄ an advertisement for a meeting for parents on 22 March at 10am at the setting. Its purpose is to organise a teddy bear's picnic in two months, as both a social occasion and to raise funds. Put in your portfolio.

➤ *P9.1*: 1, cross- . . . . . Enlarge the poster to A3 size and repeat the exercise, using the extra space for ◄
reference to **M1** additional information.

➤ *P9.1*: 1, 2, 3, 4, 5 . . .

Case study

A parents' group meets every Tuesday morning to learn about and discuss ◄ different aspects of the setting, play activities, childcare and education issues. Over recent months the numbers have been dropping and a re-launch has been planned to encourage new members to join. Everyone has been asked to take whatever opportunities they can to inform the parents of this group and its activities. How will you approach this issue? When and how will you raise the subject? How will you respond to requests for more information? Write down the case study with your responses for your portfolio.

Follow on

Find out from your setting the various methods that have been used to inform parents about group meetings. If relevant, photograph noticeboards, particularly if you have been involved in their presentation, and put in your portfolio.

Gaining your NVQ Level 2 in Early Years Care and Education

early years
training & management

Questions
(See answer pointers at end of chapter.)

➤ **1.** *What are the barriers to effective communication with parents?* · · · · · · · · · · **P9.1**: 3 ◄

➤ **2.** *There are two main types of question: open questions and closed questions.* · · · · **P9.1**: 5 ◄
How do you differentiate between the two? Give examples.

➤ **3.** *If you felt unable to answer a parent's enquiry relating to a group meeting in* · · · **P9.1**: 6 ◄
the setting, who would you refer to?

Record the questions and your full answers and share these with your assessor.

Did you know?
The *Curriculum Guidance for the Foundation Stage* (QCA, 2001) recognises the vital role parents have to play in the care and education of their children. It states that effective teaching requires 'Working in partnership with parents, because parents continue to have a prime teaching role with their children'.

Extra ideas
Using the 'Spider chart' photocopiable sheet on page 122, write 'Inform parents about group' in the centre. In each of the surrounding boxes write one method of communicating information. Put in your portfolio.

Element P9.2 Encourage parents to participate in group functions

➤ Your assessor can observe and question you. · **P9.2**: Range 1a, b, 2a, ◄
b, c, d, 3a, b, c

Organising a group meeting

Resources
Suitable room; furniture; refreshments; 'Meeting plan' photocopiable sheet on page 142.

Preparation
Complete the 'Meeting plan' sheet. Ensure parents have been notified of the event. Check the room is available and ready to be set up. Lay out the refreshments.

What to do
➤ Make the room as inviting as possible. Pay attention to the heating, lighting, cleanliness and type of furniture.
➤ Display posters or children's work if appropriate.
➤ Welcome the parents as they come in.
➤ Introduce the parents to each other and inform them that you would like them to join in any discussions.
➤ Try to find out the parents' interests and skills.
➤ Involve the parents in offering refreshments, especially those new to the group.
➤ Thank all the parents for coming and tidy up after they leave.

Tip

➤ Both parents and staff may feel nervous at being involved in a group. Recognising this helps.

Support and extension

The arrangement of the furniture can reflect the type of meeting being held. For less formal groups arrange the chairs in a circle so everyone can be involved. For formal meetings you may need to sit around a table or in rows if there are many people.

Evaluation

Was everything ready for the group to meet? Would you do anything differently next time? Were you comfortable working with a group of parents?

Supporting activity

➤ **P9.2**: 2, 7 · · · · · · · To enable parents to join a group meeting during the day, you may need to set up a crèche for their babies and toddlers. Use the 'Notice' photocopiable sheet on page 141 to draw up a poster promoting the crèche. Emphasise the opportunity it will give parents to participate in the group. Put the poster in your portfolio.

Case study

➤ **P9.2**: 1, 2, 3, 4, 5, · · · 6, 7

The Tuesday morning parents' group is proving to be very successful. Parents attend to learn about and discuss different aspects of the setting, play activities, and discuss child care and education issues. You assist in this group, provide activities and resources, and join in where appropriate. What are the strategies you could use to encourage participation in group functions? Write down the case study with your responses for your portfolio.

Follow on

Identify the areas that might be raised or discussed in a parental group in your setting.

Questions

(See answer pointers at end of chapter.)

➤ **P9.2**: 1, 2, 3, 6 · · · · **4.** *How can you encourage parents to interact with each other?*

➤ **P9.2**: 3 · · · · · · · · **5.** *List ten types of group meetings that may support parents and childcare and early years settings?*

➤ **P9.2**: 7 · · · · · · · · **6.** *Suggest barriers that may prevent parents from participating in groups?*

Record the questions and your full answers and share these with your assessor.

Did you know?

A three-year-old's brain is three times more active than a teenager's.

➤ **P9.2**: 4, 5, 6 · · · · · · **Extra idea**

List the skills and interests that parents may be able to bring to support group functions, including language skills and knowledge of cultural diversity.

Element P9.3 Encourage parents to participate in children's activities

➤ Your assessor can observe and question you. · ◄ **P9.3**: Range 1a, b, c, d, 2b

One potato, two potato

Parents can enjoy this activity with their children in a setting or at home.
Number of children: four.

Resources
Potatoes; sharp paring knife (adult use); paint; plastic vegetable tray; kitchen paper; different-coloured paper; aprons.

Preparation
Plan the activity using the 'Activity preparation' photocopiable sheet on page 121. Ask your setting supervisor for support in doing this if necessary. Scrub and dry the potatoes.

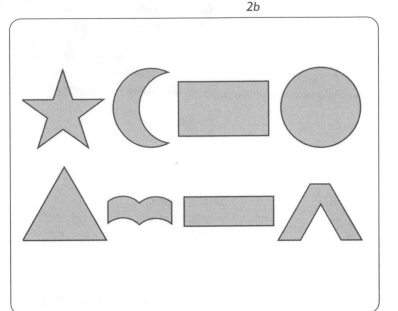

What to do
➤ Show the parents how to cut the potatoes in half and, with care, cut out sections of the flat side to make printing shapes (see illustration for shape ideas).
➤ Invite the parents to make paint pads by folding the kitchen paper to form a pad to fit the bottom of the vegetable tray. Pour a thin layer of paint over it.
➤ Help the children to put aprons on.
➤ Let the children and parents press the flat side of the potato firmly on to the paint pad and use to print several times on to the paper.
➤ Encourage the children to use one shape for each colour.
➤ Let the children choose the shape and colour of the prints and paper.
➤ Praise and encourage the children.
➤ Remind the parents that the end result is not as important as the opportunity to take part, to experiment and to achieve. The adult's role is to provide materials, observe, encourage and support language development and learning.
➤ Help the children to tidy the area and display the prints.

✔ **Tip**

➤ By ensuring that a mix of new and established parents, some active participants and others less sure, come to a group, you can cover the Parents' Range category in this Element.

Support and extension
➤ Straight-sided shapes are easier to cut out of the potatoes than curves. Extend the activity by offering different fruits and vegetables to print with, such as apple halves, carrot circles and half a small cabbage.

Cross-reference to **C9** ◄

Evaluation
Did you welcome the parents to the activity? Did you show them how to prepare for printing? Did you encourage the parents to let the children make their own choices and to supervise rather than help? Did you show, by your practice, how to talk to the children about the activity, about colours, shapes, potatoes, vegetables in general and cooking? Did you introduce new words, such as 'triangle', 'print', 'press' and 'grip'?

P9.3: 3 · · · · · · · ·

Supporting activity

Design a booklet for parents showing which activities the children take part in at the setting that they can do at home with their children. Identify the purpose and the aims of the activity and how the parents can participate.

P9.3: 1, 2, 3, 4, 5, · · · 6, 7

Case study

On several occasions each year the parents who attend the Tuesday Group are invited to take part in activities with the children in the main setting. You are expected to assist in this. What do you think your role will be? How can you encourage parental participation and how do you see yourself doing it? Write down the case study with your responses for your portfolio.

Follow on

Keep a list of parents who have helped with activities in your setting, noting the sorts of activities they feel most comfortable with. They may need encouragement to try other things and you can offer your support.

Questions

(See answer pointers at end of chapter.)

P9.3: 1 · · · · · · · · ·

7. How can you actively stimulate the parents' interest to become involved in the children's activities?

P9.3: 3, 4, 5 · · · · · ·

8. What opportunities are there for you to identify, match and use the parents' own interests?

P9.3: 6, 7 · · · · · · ·

9. How can you encourage inhibited parents to actively engage in activities with the children?

Record the questions and your full answers and share these with your assessor.

Did you know?

According to the *National Numeracy Strategy* (DfES, 2002) the Education Department expects that 'parents are kept well-informed and encouraged to be involved through discussions at school and sometimes in work with pupils at home'.

P9.3: 4 · · · · · · · ·

Extra idea

Make a collection of multicultural activities and ask the parents to share their diverse experiences with the setting.

Practical ways of collecting evidence

If you are involved with parents in groups, keep a log book of basic information, such as the purpose of the group, where is it held, how many parents attend, what your role is and a brief evaluation of your part. Share your log book with your assessor, who may question you. Photocopy a page and put in your portfolio.

Check your progress

For this Unit you are expected to be directly observed by your assessor for at least one aspect of each Range category for each of the three Elements. You can cover more than one aspect if the opportunity arises. For any of the Range statements or Performance Criteria not observed, evidence can be collected by other means. If you have been involved in the preparation, you can include posters, leaflets and booklets giving written information for parents about groups and activities, programmes of activities and photographs and plans to show parents what happens in the setting. Evidence can be gained from reflective accounts of your practice and evaluation of your personal effectiveness in working with groups, matching parents' skills and interests and encouraging them to participate. Witness statements from colleagues and parents can be included, as well as other evidence, such as records, case studies and transferable skills from other work with children and parents.

Answer pointers

Ensure your answers are fully made for your assessor.

1. Language. Sensory impairment. Illiteracy. Dyslexia. Time constraints.

2. Requiring yes/no response. Questions allowing fuller answers/choice. Do you like milk? How do you feel about that?

3. Supervisor. Colleague. Committee member. Head of setting.

4. Introductions. Share tasks. Common interests. Support one another.

5. Management committee. Fundraising. Coffee mornings. Outings. Parenting classes.

6. Need childcare for siblings. Language. Working. Disability. Over committed. Transport.

7. Make feel welcome. Enthusiasm. Within abilities. Support. Interesting activities. Special place. Appreciated. Show photographs. Displays. Thank.

8. Conversation. Discussions. Link to home. Records. Observation.

9. Encourage. Support. Level of participation. Select activity carefully. Give choice. Pair with parent. Pair with practitioner.

Further information

Managing to Change – Training Materials for Staff in Day Care Centres for Young Children: Partnership with Parents
Liz Cowley
(National Children's Bureau, 1995)

A Practical Guide to Activities for Young Children
Christine Hobart and Jill Frankel
(Nelson Thornes, 1999)

CU10 Contribute to the effectiveness of work teams

This Unit recognises the practitioner's contribution to teamwork. This includes teams working closely together and loosely structured teams. A team is defined as members who work together with the same aims to meet the needs of individual children.

The first Element looks at effective team working through appropriate behaviour, passing on relevant information, receiving and acting on constructive feedback and improving team practice. You are expected to seek advice over problems within the team, whether clashes of personality, confusion over roles or inappropriate behaviour such as bullying, discrimination or harassment.

The second Element focuses on self-reflection: assessing competence, capability and development. The Unit is designed for those who work as part of a team but without line management responsibility for that team.

This chapter will enable you to:
CU10.1 Contribute to effective team working
CU10.2 Develop oneself in own work role.

Element CU10.1 Contribute to effective team working

➤ *CU10.1: Range 1b, c, d*

Your assessor can observe and question you.

Communication pointers
Team working is about everyone playing a part and communicating effectively. Below are suggestions for effective communication.

What to do
➤ Write clearly to ensure others can read and understand.
➤ Listen to others.
➤ Keep your colleagues informed as to where you will be at certain times and what you will be doing. This is important if you have arranged with a colleague to do certain tasks or will be out of the play area.
➤ Give clear guidance and instruction to the children.
➤ Suggest changes to the room layout or additional activities.
➤ Act on feedback from colleagues.
➤ Put right misunderstandings.
➤ Respect another person's viewpoint – this does not mean you have to agree with them.
➤ Learn to read non-verbal communication, facial gestures, eye contact, body movements, touch, posture and personal space.
➤ Avoid offence and conflict by thinking before acting.

early years
*training &
management*

➤ Reflect on information that has been given to you to show that you understand.
➤ Use anti-discriminatory, non-stereotypical, positive language.
➤ Keep calm when you are criticised.
➤ Apologise when you are wrong.
➤ Offer assistance in a friendly and helpful way.
➤ Diffuse conflict by keeping calm and not overreacting.
➤ Be aware of cultural differences in body language and speech patterns.
➤ Consider who you are talking to and adjust your language accordingly.

> ✓ **Tip**
>
> ➤ A team only works if everyone plays their part.

Support and extension
Communication is a two-way process. You need to communicate with adults and children, and they need to communicate with you. To be an effective team player you need to practise these skills to improve.

Evaluation
Do you think you are an effective communicator? Could you benefit by receiving training in some aspects? Are you afraid to speak to senior colleagues? Do your written skills let you down? Are you comfortable talking to parents? Do you communicate well with children?

Supporting activity
Write a chart showing all the members of the team in your setting. Consider their roles and share your thoughts with your assessor.

➤ | **Case study**
You have a large collection of fir cones from a friend's tree and have an idea for making them into animal shapes with the children. There are enough for all the groups in the setting, including the out-of-school club. How will you raise this idea with your colleagues? What will you ask of them? What are the consequences of this action likely to be? Write down the case study with your responses for your portfolio.

CU10.1: 1, 2, 3, 4 ◄

➤ | **Follow on**
If your contribution is included in the minutes of a meeting, put a copy in your portfolio with your name and contribution highlighted.

CU10.1: 7 ◄

Questions
(See answer pointers at end of chapter.)
➤ **1.** *In what ways do humans communicate? Give examples.* · · · · · · · · · · **CU10.1**: 1, 2, 3, 4, 5, ◄
7, 8
➤ **2.** *What, in your opinion, is a suitable dress code for early years practitioners?* · · · · **CU10.1**: 2 ◄
➤ **3.** *In a work context, what is meant by 'interpersonal problems'?* · · · · · · · · · **CU10.1**: 9 ◄

Record the questions and your full answers and share these with your assessor.

Did you know?

According to John Humphries, in *Managing Through People* (How To Books, 1999), analysis of successful teams show shared common features, such as a common purpose, interaction, a strong sense of identity, small teams, a code of behaviour, high levels of mutual support and an internal structure where certain roles are taken by team members according to likes and abilities.

Extra ideas

➤ **CU10.1**: *1, 2, 3, 7* · · ·   ◄ Imagine a new member of staff is to start at your setting. Draw up an induction programme to familiarise them with the team set up. Describe roles and responsibilities, management structures (who reports to who, where to get support from, who to keep informed and when), how information is passed on to staff, team meetings, how staff rotas work and any specific details relating to your team. Put your notes in your portfolio.

➤ **CU10.1**: *2, 3, 4, 5, 7* · · ·   ◄ Using the 'Spider chart' photocopiable sheet on page 122, write 'Skills required for effective teamwork' in the centre. In each surrounding box write positive aspects that help the team to function, such as co-operation, support and respecting others.

➤ **CU10.1**: *1, 2, 3, 4,* · · ·   ◄ Use the following list to record how you have been an effective team member:
5, 6, 7, 8, 9

- ◆ Informed others of activities I was involved in.
- ◆ Information and ideas passed to a team member.
- ◆ Accepted suggestions and information.
- ◆ Offered assistance.
- ◆ Did what I agreed to.
- ◆ Made suggestions to team members.
- ◆ Dealt with a difference of opinion.
- ◆ Sought advice over problems with team members.

Element CU10.2 Develop oneself in own work role

➤ **CU10.2**: *Range 1a, b*   ◄ Your assessor can observe and question you.

Skills audit

Everyone has particular skills and interests. It is helpful to think through individual's strengths to increase confidence and identify weaknesses. We are then better placed to work on and improve our skills.

What to do

➤ List the interests and skills required to work with young children. Add to these the skills you use in your setting, such as:

- ◆ Story telling
- ◆ A language other than English
- ◆ Caring for babies
- ◆ Communicating with children
- ◆ Providing imaginative play
- ◆ Including multicultural ideas in play

- ♦ Natural materials and environmental play
- ♦ Displays
- ♦ Caring for animals
- ♦ Art and craft
- ♦ Music
- ♦ Physical activities
- ♦ Explaining how things work
- ♦ Organisational skills.

Tip

➤ A good team member thinks of the implications of their actions on others. Teams are organic. It is the responsibility of all members to continue their personal development to meet the changing needs of the team.

Support and extension
Give yourself a score between one and three for each entry. This will indicate where you can benefit from additional support. Discuss with your supervisor, asking for feedback on your work practice in these areas. Your assessor can observe the feedback session.

Evaluation
Childcare and early years practitioners should evaluate their work. This does not need to be a formal evaluation, but it is useful to make a mental note of what works, what needs changing, how to make it more challenging or simple. For feedback to be valuable you need to act on it.

Supporting activity
➤ Having identified where you can benefit from additional support, think of ways to achieve it. Complete the 'Action plan' photocopiable sheet on page 143. You can do this with your supervisor.

CU10.2: 1, 2, 3 ◄

Case study
➤ A new person is managing the setting and staff have been asked to introduce themselves, describe their role and suggest ways to develop it. How will you describe your role and the ways it can be developed? How will that fit in with the team? What are your career ambitions? Write down the case study with your responses for your portfolio.

CU10.2: 1, 2, 3 ◄

Follow on
Investigate career options and where you may go when you have gained your NVQ award.

Questions
(See answer pointers at end of chapter.)

➤ **4.** *What would your personal development objectives be and how will you ensure they are met?*

CU10.2: 2 ◄

➤ **5.** *In what ways can you take responsibility for your own development, learning and performance?*

CU10.2: 3 ◄

➤ **6.** *What forms of feedback might you receive from your colleagues, supervisor, parents, tutor or assessor? Give examples.*

CU10.2: 4 ◄

Record the questions and your full answers and share these with your assessor.

Did you know?

According to the *Housewife Baby Book* (1948), a working mother could employ a college-trained nurse in the home, from a recognised Nursery Training School, with at least 18 months' training, for a recommended pay of £85 per year plus board, lodging and her employer's superannuation contribution. The nurse can expect her salary to reach £260.

➤ *CU10.2*: 1, 2 · · · · · · ·

Extra idea

Complete the 'Reflective account' photocopiable sheet on page 144 about an activity you have carried out. Explain what you did, think through any changes to accommodate all children, identify what you have learned and note the gaps in your knowledge. Note examples of your responsibilities on a copy of your job description.

Practical ways of collecting evidence

Demonstrate how you work within a team. There will be many opportunities to receive instruction, carry out requests, assist others, make suggestions and carry out your duties.

Check your progress

Your assessor must directly observe you in real activities for each Element in this Unit. Working in teams is a common factor throughout the NVQ process, so evidence will have already been gained through direct observations as you progress through the award. You must provide evidence for all the Performance Criteria and all aspects of the Range categories, although **CU10.1**: Range 2 may not be observed. In this event, you will need to find evidence from other sources, such as work products (inspection reports identifying the workings of the team), personal records, witness testimonies, questioning, reflective accounts of your practice, case studies and, for the knowledge specification, assignments and projects. Simulations are not considered appropriate evidence for this Unit.

Answer pointers

Ensure your answers are fully made for your assessor.
1. Written. Verbal. Body language. Tone of voice. Facial expressions. Gestures. Sign language.
2. Sensible footwear. Stud earrings. Long hair tied back. Modest clothing. No chunky jewellery.
3. Personality clashes. Harassment. Racism. Bullying. Discrimination. Undermining
4. Work effectively in a team. Improve practice. Offer a better service. Realistic. Challenging. Achievable.
5. Listen to and act on feedback. Use initiative. Ask questions. Request training.
6. Written. Verbal. Non verbal, through gestures and body language.

Further information

Caring For Young Children
Lance and Jennie Lindon (Macmillan, 1994)

Self-management and Personal Effectiveness
Julie-Ann Amos (How To Books, 1999)

Activity preparation

Activity

Who will be doing it?

Resources required

Comments

Spider chart

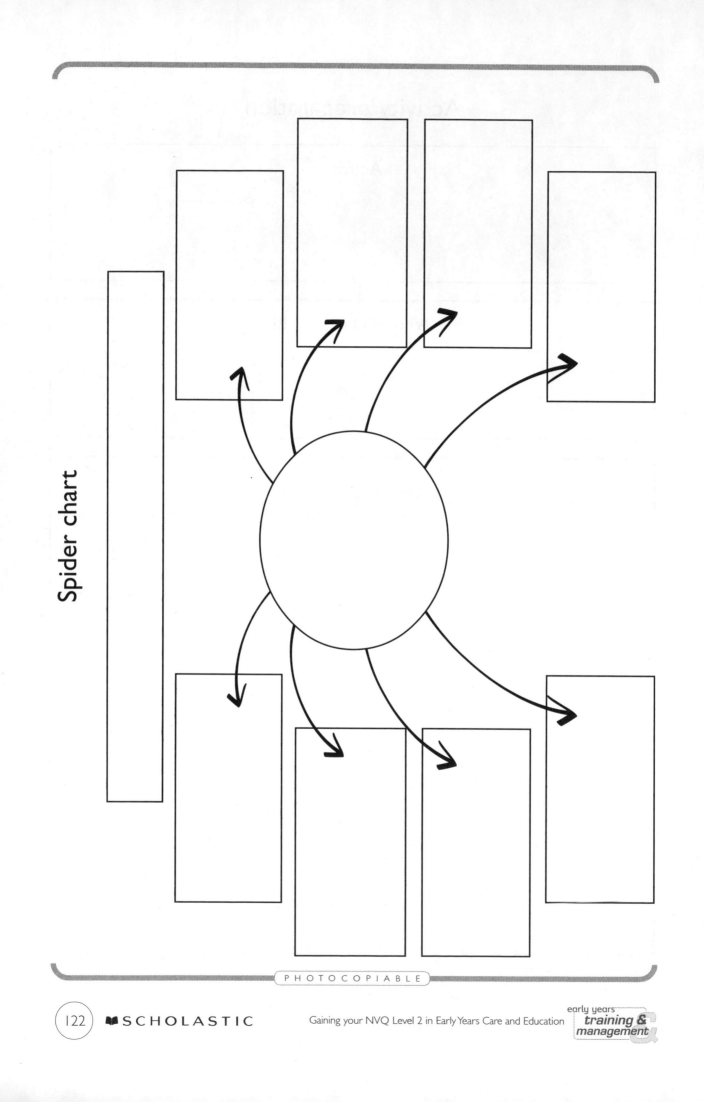

Behaviour game

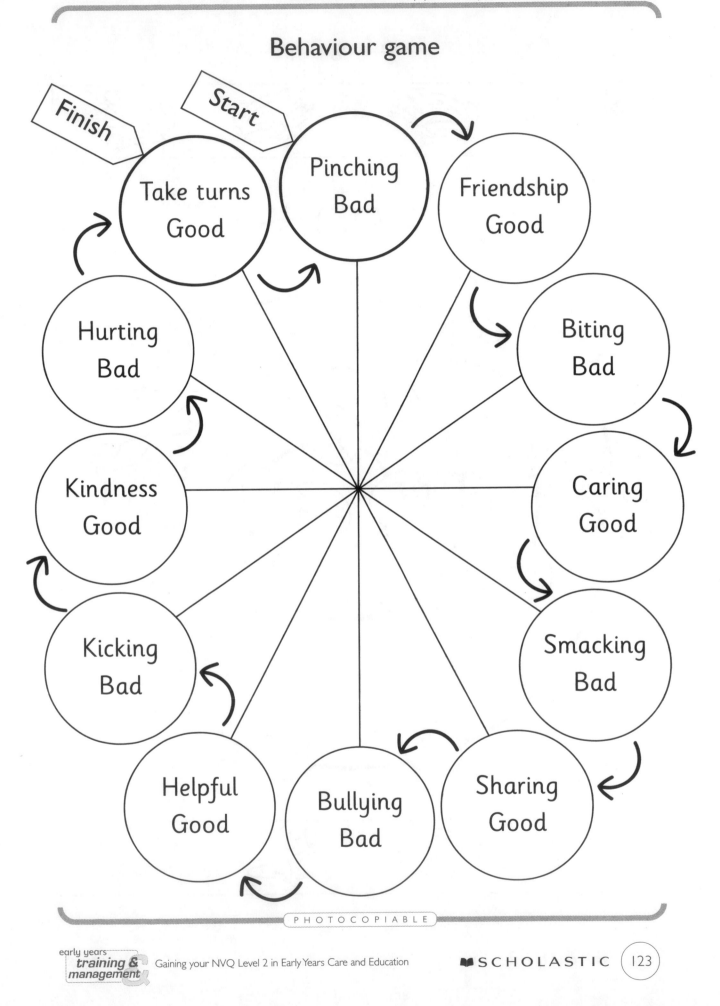

Hop frog hop

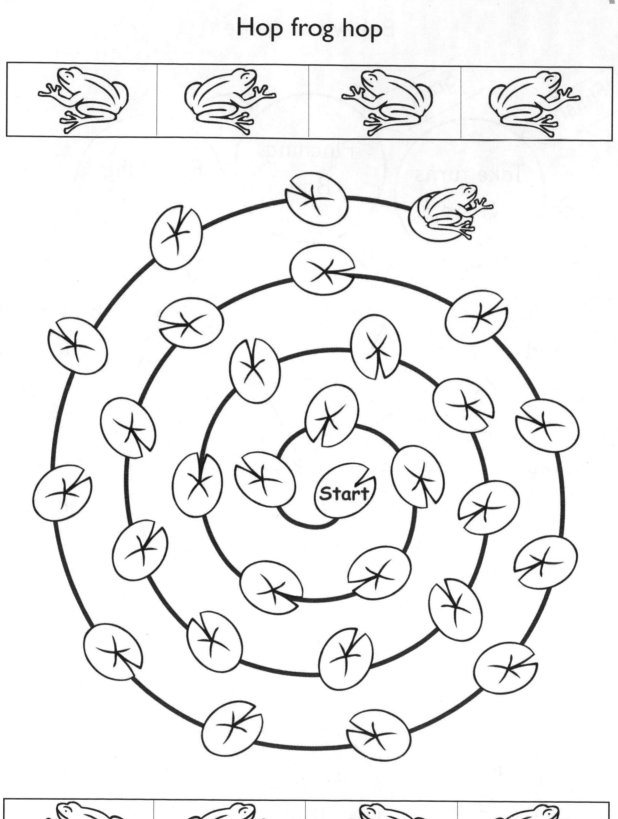

SCHOLASTIC Gaining your NVQ Level 2 in Early Years Care and Education

early years
*training &
management*

Easy recipes

Hot milk and a chocolate spoon

Milk chocolate
Sugar strands
Heavy plastic spoons
Cup of milk per child
Marshmallows

■ Melt the chocolate in a bowl over a saucepan of hot water.
■ Dip the spoon into the chocolate to cover both sides of the bowl of the spoon.
■ Allow to cool on greaseproof paper for five minutes, then dip into a saucer of sugar strands.
■ Warm milk in the cup and float a marshmallow in it.
■ Stir with the chocolate spoon.

Chocolate squares

400g condensed milk
200g digestive biscuits
1tsp vanilla essence
100g milk chocolate
Cherries

■ Place biscuits in a plastic bag and crush with a rolling pin.
■ Place in bowl and add vanilla essence, condensed milk and melted chocolate.
■ Put mixture in a greased 20cm square baking tin and place in a cool place to set.
■ Cut into small squares and decorate each one with a cherry.

Strawberry mousse

Strawberry jelly
1½ tbsp cornflour
1tbsp sugar
½tsp strawberry flavouring
275ml milk
Fresh strawberries

■ Dissolve the jelly in 275ml boiling water and leave to set.
■ Make a sauce by mixing cornflour with a little milk in a jug. Heat the rest of milk with the sugar and stir into cornflour mix. Return to pan and cook until it thickens, stirring continuously. Add the flavouring.
■ Allow to cool.
■ Crush strawberries with a fork, reserving some whole ones for decoration. Stir into the cold set sauce.
■ Whip jelly until frothy and fold into sauce.
■ Spoon into serving dishes and decorate with whole strawberries.

Potato fluff

Whole potato
Butter
Cheese
Chives
Baked beans

■ Scrub the potato well and prick with a fork.
■ Place in the microwave for six minutes, or until it is soft in the middle when tested.
■ Put on one side to cool.
■ Grate the cheese.
■ Cut the potato in half and scrape out the soft potato centre, leaving the skins intact.
■ Mash the potato, cheese and butter together.
■ Stir in the chopped chives.
■ Pile back into the potato shells and reheat for one minute.
■ Warm the beans and serve with the potato.

Play dough recipes

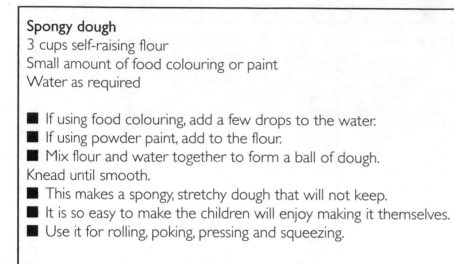

Spongy dough
3 cups self-raising flour
Small amount of food colouring or paint
Water as required

- If using food colouring, add a few drops to the water.
- If using powder paint, add to the flour.
- Mix flour and water together to form a ball of dough.
Knead until smooth.
- This makes a spongy, stretchy dough that will not keep.
- It is so easy to make the children will enjoy making it themselves.
- Use it for rolling, poking, pressing and squeezing.

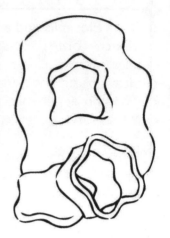

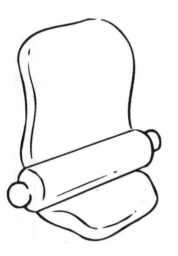

Two-way play dough
3 cups self-raising flour
3 cups salt
Water as required

- Mix salt and flour with enough water to make a non-sticky dough.
- Due to the high salt content it will feel gritty to the touch. The salt acts as a preservative and the dough will keep for up to a month in a box in the fridge.
- In this state the play dough makes a good modelling material.
- For long-lasting models bake in a cool oven for three to four hours.
- Can be painted when completely dry.

Long-lasting play dough
2 cups plain flour
1 cup salt
1 tbsp cooking oil
2 tsp cream of tartar
2 cups water
Few drops of food colouring

- Mix dry ingredients in a bowl and add oil.
- Add food colouring to water, pour in and mix well.
- Microwave on high for about three minutes, stirring every minute until the dough is dry.

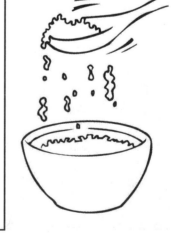

A walk in the woods

Suggestions

One day Joseph decided to go for a walk in the woods. He put on his coat and big boots and walked down the road, with a clomp, clomp, clomp.	Tap two wooden blocks together.
He came to the woods where the path was wet and his boots stuck in the mud, with a slurp, slurp, slurp.	Hand tap on a tambour.
He stopped and listened to the woodpecker searching for his breakfast in a tree, with a tap, tap, tap.	Quick finger taps.
A little further on he saw a beautiful butterfly showing her brilliant wings, with a flutter, flutter, flutter.	Triangle.
A long way off he could hear the beautiful singing of the Bell bird, with a tinkle, tinkle, tinkle.	Jingle bells.
Suddenly the sky began to get dark. In the distance he heard a rumble of thunder, with a boom, boom, boom.	Bang a drum.
He heard the rain starting, with a swish, swish, swish.	Rain stick.
Before long the rain came down, with a patter, patter, patter.	Maracas.
Not wanting to get wet, he ran home down the muddy path, with a slurp, slurp, slurp.	Hand tap on a tambour.
And back along the road, with a clomp, clomp, clomp.	Tap two wooden blocks together.
Until he shut his front door, with a BANG!	Cymbals.

PHOTOCOPIABLE

Menu

Menu

	Price
Sandwiches	
Cakes	Price
Fruit	Price
Biscuits	Price
Tea	Price
Coffee	Price

Story aids

woman

man

girl

boy

tree

dog

cat

Setting checklist

Check	Tick	Comment
Have you read your setting's health and safety policy?		
Is the area comfortable and welcoming?		
Is there room to move between the tables and other furniture?		
Is the furniture a suitable size for the children?		
Are the fire doors unobstructed?		
Check the room temperature. Is it comfortable? Play areas should be between 15°C/59°F and 18°C/64°F; baby rooms should be between 20°C/68°F and 22°C/72°F.		
Is there adequate light – natural and artificial?		
Is the room well ventilated? Do the windows open?		
Has electrical equipment been checked? When?		
Are there safety covers on electrical sockets?		
Is there toughened glass in doors and windows?		
Are there fireguards and radiator covers?		
Are there smoke alarms and fire extinguishers?		
Is the floor covering non-slip and easy to clean?		
Is there a safe surface under large outdoor play equipment?		
Are the gates well secured?		
Are the bins out of the children's reach?		

Round robin

Gaining your NVQ Level 2 in Early Years Care and Education

SCHOLASTIC 131

999

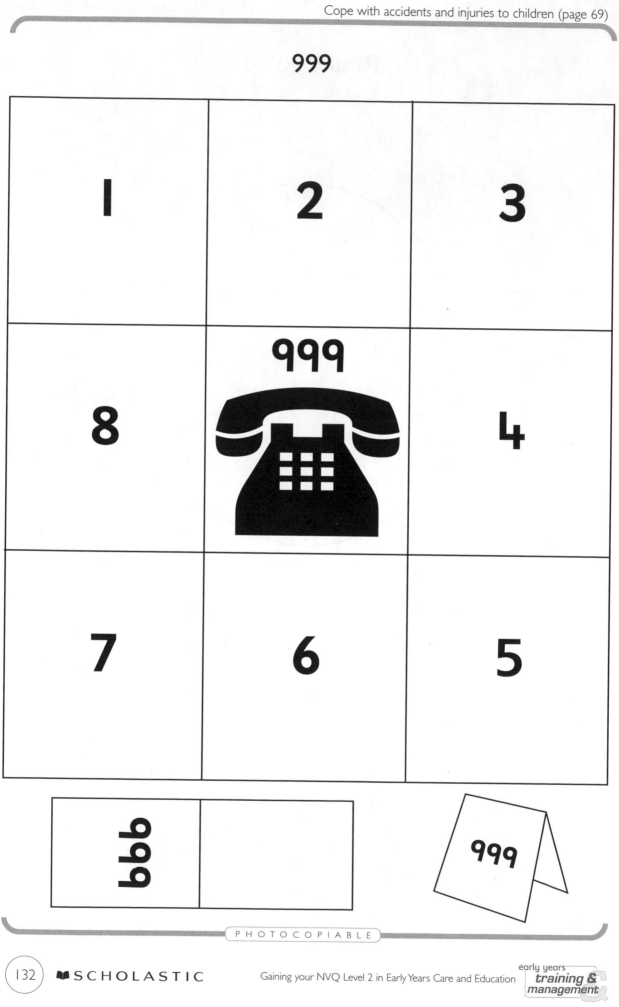

1	2	3
8	999	4
7	6	5

999

999

◼SCHOLASTIC   Gaining your NVQ Level 2 in Early Years Care and Education   early years **training & management**

Skeleton

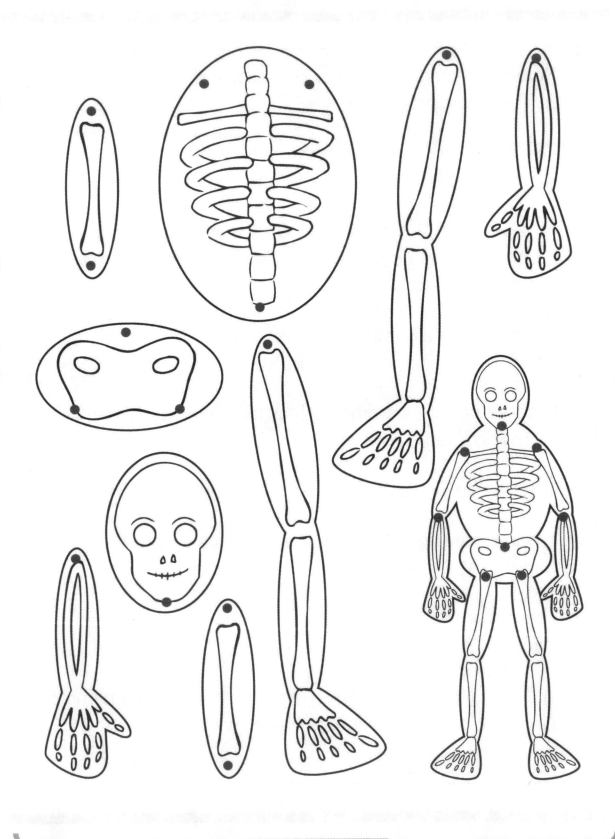

Tips for naming names

➤ Remember, names are very personal and special to all of us. They identify who we are.

➤ Use preferred names, with the correct pronunciation. It is very important to the identity of both the child and parent.

➤ Find out what the parent and child want to be called. Write their names down phonetically if you have difficulty remembering them.

➤ Do not make assumptions by referring to 'Christian' names. Parents may not be Christian.

➤ In some naming systems, such as the Chinese, the family name may come first.

➤ In some families, everyone will have a different name.

➤ In some naming systems, women may take both the husband's first and second name.

➤ Some women keep their own names as well as their husband's.

➤ In the Sikh naming system, men often take on the name of 'Singh' and women the name of 'Kaur', with or without the family name.

Play activities

Play dough helps children:

➤ To manipulate, using fine motor skills

➤ To increase concentration

➤ To release emotions

➤ To make familiar shapes, such as food and animals

➤ To choose which tools to use

➤ To express their creativity

➤ To use new words.

Books enable children:

➤ To understand the world

➤ To extend language development

➤ To listen carefully and concentrate

➤ To learn mathematical concepts, such as counting

➤ To express ideas and feelings

➤ To explore words and sounds.

Role-play enables children:

➤ To make sense of society

➤ In their social interaction

➤ To use their imagination

➤ To act out situations

➤ To develop many skills

➤ To learn about size, shape and matching

➤ To use large and small equipment.

Interest tables help children:

➤ To learn about the world

➤ To investigate objects

➤ To match similar objects

➤ To make discoveries

➤ To learn new words

➤ To use their senses

➤ To satisfy their curiosity.

Baby games

Tactile toys

➤ Make an odd sock into a tactile toy.

➤ Place a bunch of bells into the toe, fastening a rubber band around the foot of the sock behind them.

➤ In the heel section, put a piece of Cellophane paper, again fastening the section off with a rubber band.

➤ In the leg area place a squashy ball and stitch the top of the sock to hold the contents in.

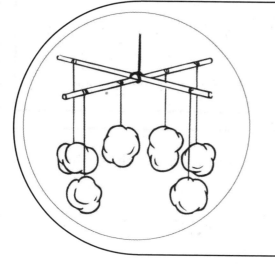

Making mobiles

➤ Make a mobile using two garden canes, crossed and tied together in the centre.

➤ Hang strips of crêpe paper tied in bundles from the canes.

➤ Hang above the baby, but out of reach.

Rice rattle

➤ Make a set of rattles from small, empty plastic drink bottles.

➤ Place a couple of spoonfuls of rice in one, pasta in another and breakfast cereal in the third.

➤ Screw the caps on tightly and seal with colourful electrical insulation tape.

PHOTOCOPIABLE

Baby menu

	Breakfast	Snack	Lunch	Tea	Supper
Monday					
Tuesday					
Wednesday					
Thursday					
Friday					

PHOTOCOPIABLE

Equipment checklist

Equipment	Date checked	Date checked	Date checked	Date checked
Cots				
High chairs				
Play pen				
Machine washable toys				
Washable toys				

◼ SCHOLASTIC   Gaining your NVQ Level 2 in Early Years Care and Education   early years training & management

Cinema role-play

Greeting card

Made especially for you by:

■SCHOLASTIC   Gaining your NVQ Level 2 in Early Years Care and Education   early years training & management

Notice

Meeting plan

Who needs to be informed?

Book and check environment (room, chairs, tables)

Resources needed?

Notes

Action plan

Skills/activity	Support/training required	Who by?	When?

early years
training &
management

Gaining your NVQ Level 2 in Early Years Care and Education

SCHOLASTIC

Develop oneself in own work role (page 119)

Reflective account

Describe activity/session

What part did I play?

Did it work or would I change anything?

Are there ways to adapt the activity/session to accommodate children of different developmental levels?

What did I learn on this occasion?

What more do I need to find out?

▮ SCHOLASTIC   Gaining your NVQ Level 2 in Early Years Care and Education   early years *training & management*